Complete Study Edition

Julius Caesar

Commentary | Complete Text | Glossary

edited by

SIDNEY LAMB

Associate Professor of English,
Sir George Williams University, Montreal

Cliffs Notes
INCORPORATED

LINCOLN, NEBRASKA 68501

Julius Caesar

SHAKESPEARE WAS NEVER MORE MEANINGFUL—

. . . than when read in Cliff's "Complete Study Edition." The introductory sections give you all of the background information about the author and his work necessary for reading with understanding and appreciation. A descriptive bibliography provides guidance in the selection of works for further study. The inviting three-column arrangement of the complete text offers the maximum in convenience to the reader. Adjacent to the text there is a running commentary that provides clear supplementary discussion of the play as it develops. Obscure words and obsolete usages used by Shakespeare are explained in the glosses directly opposite to the line in which they occur. The numerous allusions are also clarified.

SIDNEY LAMB—

. . . the editor of this Shakespeare "Complete Study Edition," attended Andover Academy and Columbia University, receiving the Prince of Wales Medal for Philosophy and the Moyes Travelling Fellowship. Following graduate studies in Elizabethan literature at King's College, Cambridge, from 1949 to 1952, he became a member of the English Faculty of the University of London's University of the Gold Coast in West Africa. Professor Lamb joined the faculty of Sir George Williams University, Montreal, in 1956.

Julius Caesar

Contents

th bene fundry times publiquely
ght Honourable the Lord Cham
his Seruants.

THE MOST EX-
cellent and lamentable
Tragedie, of Romeo
and *Iuliet.*

an introduction

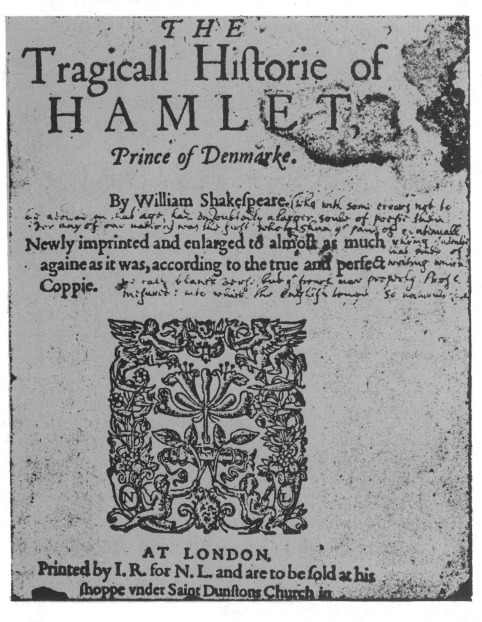

THE
Tragicall Historie of
HAMLET,
Prince of Denmarke.

By William Shakespeare.

Newly imprinted and enlarged to almost as much
againe as it was, according to the true and perfect
Coppie.

AT LONDON,
Printed by I. R. for N. L. and are to be fold at his
fhoppe vnder Saint Dunftons Church in

Two books are essential to the library of any English-speaking household; one of these is the Bible and the other is the works of William Shakespeare. These books form part of the house furnishings, not as reading material generally, but as the symbols of religion and culture—sort of a twentieth-century counterpart of the ancient Roman household gods. This symbolic status has done a great deal of damage both to religion and to Shakespeare.

Whatever Shakespeare may have been, he was not a deity. He was a writer of popular plays, who made a good living, bought a farm in the country, and retired at the age of about forty-five to enjoy his profits as a gentleman. The difference between Shakespeare and the other popular playwrights of his time was that he wrote better plays —plays that had such strong artistic value that they have been popular ever since. Indeed, even today, if Shakespeare could col-

William to Shakespeare

lect his royalties, he would be among the most prosperous of playwrights.

During the eighteenth century but mostly in the nineteenth, Shakespeare's works became "immortal classics," and the cult of Shakespeare-worship was inaugurated. The plays were largely removed from their proper place on the stage into the library where they became works of literature rather than drama and were regarded as long poems, attracting all the artistic and psuedo-artistic atmosphere surrounding poetry. In the nineteenth century this attitude was friendly but later, and especially in the early twentieth century, a strange feeling arose in the English-speaking world that poetry was sissy stuff, not for men but for "pansies" and women's clubs. This of course is sheer nonsense.

This outline will present a detailed analysis of the play and background information which will show the play in its proper perspective. This means seeing the play in relation to the other plays, to the history of the times when they were written, and in relation to the theatrical technique required for their successful performance.

G. B. Harrison's book *Introducing Shakespeare,* published by Penguin Books, will be of value for general information about Shakespeare and his plays. For reference material on the Elizabethan Theater, consult E. K. Chambers, *The Elizabethan Theatre* (four volumes). For study of the organization and production methods of this theater see *Henslowe's Diary* edited by W. W. Greg. Again for general reading the student will enjoy Margaret Webster's *Shakespeare Without Tears,* published by Whittlesey House (McGraw-Hill) in 1942.

The remainder of the Introduction will be divided into sections discussing Shakespeare's life, his plays, and his theater.

LIFE OF WILLIAM SHAKESPEARE

From the standpoint of one whose main interest lies with the plays themselves, knowledge of Shakespeare's life is not very important. Inasmuch as it treats of the period between 1592 and 1611, when the plays were being written, knowledge of his life is useful in that it may give some clues as to the topical matters introduced into the plays. For instance, the scene of Hamlet's advice to the players (Act III Scene ii) takes on an added significance when considered along with the fame and bombastic style of Edward Alleyn, the then famous actor-manager of the Lord Admiral's Players (the most powerful rivals of Shakespeare's company).

This biography is pieced together from the surviving public records of the day, from contemporary references in print, and from the London Stationer's Register. It is by no means complete. The skeletal nature of the biographical material available to scholars has led commentators in the past to invent part of the story to fill it out. These parts have frequently been invented by men who were more interested in upholding a private theory than in telling the truth, and this habit of romancing has led to a tradition of inaccurate Shakespearian biography. For this reason this outline may be of use in disposing of bad traditions.

In the heyday of the self-made man, the story developed that Shakespeare was a poor boy from the village, virtually uneducated, who fled from Stratford to London to escape prosecution for poaching on the lands of Sir Thomas Lucy, and thereby his talent and a commendable industry raised himself to greatness. This rags-to-riches romance was in the best Horatio Alger tradition but was emphatically not true. The town records of Stratford make it clear that John Shakespeare, father of the playwright, was far from a pauper. He was a wealthy and responsible citizen who held in turn several municipal offices. He married (1557) Mary Arden, the daughter of a distinguished Catholic family. William, their third son, was baptized in the Parish Church in 1564. He had a good grammar school education. Ben Jonson's remark that Shakespeare had "small Latin and less Greek" did not mean the same in those days, when the educated man had a fluent command of

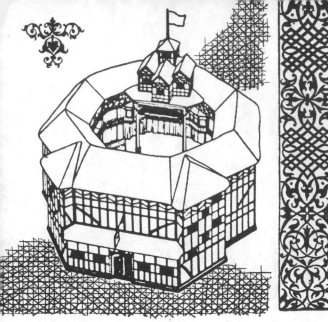

Exterior view of "The Globe"

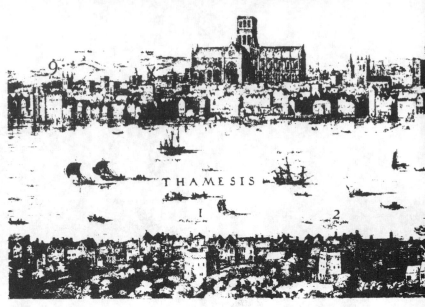

Shakespeare's London

Interior view of "The Globe"

an introduction to Shakespeare

Latin and probably at least a reading knowledge of Greek, as it does now when classical scholars are few. The remark has been construed by the Horatio Alger people as meaning that Shakespeare reached London a semiliterate bumpkin; it is nonsense. It means merely that Shakespeare was not a university man, as most of the writers were, and that the University Wits were taking out their jealousy in snobbery and pointing out that Shakespeare used less purely literary symbolism than they did.

Shakespeare married Ann Hathaway when he was eighteen years old. She was some years older than he and the marriage seems to have been a rather hasty affair. Five months after the marriage, Suzanna, the first child, was born. Two years later, in 1585, twins Hamnet and Judith were baptized.

No one knows when Shakespeare came to London. The first mention of him occurs in the bad-tempered pamphlet which Robert Greene, one of the University Wits and a famous playwright, wrote just before his death. Greene complains of "an upstart crow, beautified with our feathers, that with his tiger's heart wrapped in a player's hide, supposes he is as well able to bombast out a blank verse as the best of you; and being an absolute Yohannes factotum, is in his own conceit the only Shakescene in a country." This was written in 1592 and indicates not only that Shakespeare was in London at the time, but that he was writing plays and beginning to make such a name for himself as to call forth the jealous apprehension of an established writer.

The next year, 1593, was a year of plague, and by order of the Lord Mayor and the Aldermen, the theaters were closed. The players, disorganized by this action, went on tour outside of London. During this year Shakespeare's two long poems, *Venus and Adonis* and *The Rape of Lucrece,* were entered in the Stationer's Register. Both were dedicated to the Earl of Southampton.

The public theaters had not been established very long. The first of these, called the Theatre, was built for James Burbage in 1576. By 1594, there were three such theaters in London, the two new houses being the Curtain and the Rose. By 1594, also, the three most celebrated of the writers, Kyd, Greene, and Marlowe were dead, and Shakespeare had already a considerable reputation. Before this date the theaters had been largely low class entertainment and the plays had been of rather poor quality. Through the revival of classical drama in the schools (comedies) and the Inns of Court (tragedies), an interest had been created in the stage. The noblemen of the time were beginning to attend the public theaters, and their tastes demanded a better class of play.

Against the background of this

increasing status and upper-class popularity of the theaters, Shakespeare's company was formed. After the 1594 productions under Alleyn, this group of actors divided. Alleyn formed a company called the Lord Admiral's Company which played in Henslowe's Rose Theatre. Under the leadership of the Burbages (James was the owner of the Theatre and his son Richard was a young tragic actor of great promise), Will Kemp (the famous comedian), and William Shakespeare, the Lord Chamberlain's company came into being. This company continued throughout Shakespeare's career. It was renamed in 1603, shortly after Queen Elizabeth's death, becoming the King's players.

The company played at the Theatre until Burbage's lease on the land ran out. The landlord was not willing to come to satisfactory terms. The company moved across the river and built the new Globe theater. The principal sharers in the new place were Richard and Cuthbert Burbage each with two and a half shares and William Shakespeare, John Heminge, Angustus Phillips, Thomas Pope, and Will Kemp, each with one share.

Burbage had wanted to establish a private theater and had rented the refectory of the old Blackfriars' monastery. Not being allowed to use this building he leased it to a man called Evans who obtained permission to produce plays acted by chil-

dren. This venture was so successful as to make keen competition for the existing companies. This vogue of child actors is referred to in *Hamlet,* Act II Scene ii.

The children continued to play at Blackfriars until, in 1608, their license was suspended because of the seditious nature of one of their productions. By this time the public attitude towards the theaters had changed, and Burbage's Company, now the King's players, could move into the Blackfriars theater.

Partners with the Burbages in this enterprise were Shakespeare, Heminge, Condell, Sly, and Evans. This was an indoor theater, whereas the Globe had been outdoors. The stage conditions were thus radically altered. More scenery could be used; lighting effects were possible. Shakespeare's works written for this theater show the influence of change in conditions.

To return to the family affairs of the Shakespeares, records show that in 1596 John Shakespeare was granted a coat of arms and, along with his son, was entitled to call himself "gentleman." In this year also, William Shakespeare's son Hamnet died. In 1597 William Shakespeare bought from William Underwood a sizable estate at Stratford, called New Place.

Shakespeare's father died in 1601, his mother, in 1608. Both of his daughters married, one in 1607, the other in 1616.

During this time, Shakespeare went on acquiring property in Stratford. He retired to New Place probably around 1610 although this date is not definitely established, and his career as a dramatist was practically at an end. *The Tempest,* his last complete play, was written around the year 1611.

The famous will, in which he left his second best bed to his wife, was executed in 1616 and later on in that same year he was buried.

THE PLAYS

Thirty-seven plays are customarily included in the works of William Shakespeare. Scholars have been at great pains to establish the order in which these plays were written. The most important sources of information for this study are the various records of performances which exist, the printed editions which came out during Shakespeare's career, and such unmistakable references to current events as may crop up in the plays. The effect of the information gathered in this way is generally to establish two dates between which a given play must have been written. In *Hamlet* for instance, there is a scene in which Hamlet refers to the severe competition given to the adult actors by the vogue for children's performances. This vogue first became a serious threat to the professional companies in about 1600. In 1603 a very bad edition was published, without authorization, of *The*

Queen Elizabeth

an introduction to Shakespeare

Elizabethan types

Lute, standing cup, stoop

Tragical History of Hamlet, Prince of Denmark by William Shakespeare. These two facts indicate that *Hamlet* was written between the years of 1600 and 1603. This process fixed the order in which most of the plays were written. Those others of which no satisfactory record could be found were inserted in their logical place in the series according to the noticeable development of Shakespeare's style. In these various ways we have arrived at the following chronological listing of the plays.

1591   *Henry VI Part I*
      Henry VI Part II
      Henry VI Part III
      Richard III
      Titus Andronicus
      Love's Labour Lost
      The Two Gentlemen of Verona
      The Comedy of Errors
      The Taming of the Shrew

1594   *Romeo and Juliet*
      A Midsummer Night's Dream
      Richard II
      King John
      The Merchant of Venice

1597   *Henry IV Part I*
      Henry IV Part II
      Much Ado About Nothing
      Merry Wives of Windsor
      As You Like It
      Julius Caesar
      Henry V
      Troilus and Cressida

1601   *Hamlet*
      Twelfth Night
      Measure for Measure
      All's Well That Ends Well

      Othello

1606   *King Lear*
      Macbeth
      Timon of Athens
      Antony and Cleopatra
      Coriolanus

1609   *Pericles*

1611   *Cymbeline*
      The Winter's Tale
      The Tempest
      Henry VIII

At this point it is pertinent to review the tradition of dramatic form that had been established before Shakespeare began writing. Drama in England sprang at the outset from the miracle and morality plays of the medieval guilds. These dramatized Bible stories became increasingly less religious as time passed until finally they fell into disrepute. The next development was the writing of so-called *interludes*. These varied in character but often took the form of bawdy farce. As the renaissance gathered force in England, Roman drama began to be revived at the schools and the Inns of Court. Before long English writers were borrowing plots and conventions wholesale from the classic drama. The Italian model was the most fashionable and consequently was largely adopted, but many features of the old *interludes* still persisted, especially in plays written for the public theaters.

With the development among the nobility of a taste for the theater, a higher quality of work became in demand. Very few of

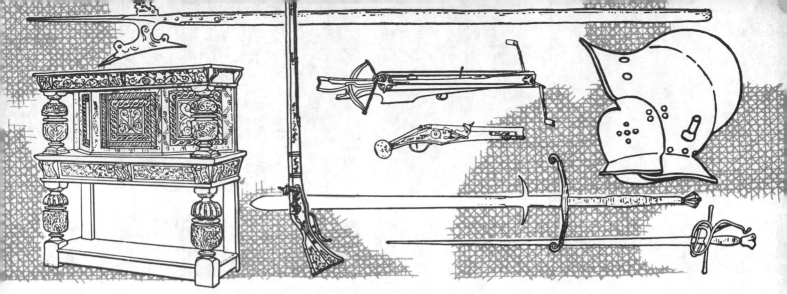

Court cupboard, crossbow, guns, sword, rapier, halberd, burgonet

the very early plays have survived. The reason for this is that the plays were not printed to be read; no one considered them worth the trouble. A play was strung together out of a set of stock characters and situations with frantic haste, often by as many as a dozen different men. These men who worked on plays did not regard their writing activity as of prime importance. They were primarily actors. With the cultivation of taste for better plays came the idea that the work of a playwright was an effort demanding special skill. The highborn audiences were interested in the plays themselves and began to include editions of their favorite plays in their libraries. With this demand for printed copies of the plays, the conception began of the dramatist as an artist in his own right, whether or not he acted himself (as most of them did).

By 1592, when Shakespeare began to make his personal reputation, a set of traditions had developed. This body of traditions gave Shakespeare the basic materials with which to work.

A special type of comedy writing had developed, centered around the name of John Lyly, designed for the sophisticated audience of the court and presented with lavish dances and decorative effects. This type of play was characterized by a delicately patterned artificiality of speech. The dialogue was studded with complicated references to Latin and Italian literature that the renaissance had made fashionable.

Shakespeare used this method extensively. In the early plays (before *The Merchant of Venice*) he was experimenting and wrote much that is nothing more than conventional. Later on, as his mature style developed, the writing becomes integral with and indispensable to the play and no longer appears artificial. In *Romeo and Juliet,* an early play, the following lines are spoken by Lady Capulet in urging Juliet to accept the Count Paris for her husband. These lines are brilliant but artificial, and the play seems to pause in order that this trick bit of word-acrobatics may be spoken.

> Read o'er the volume of young
> Paris' face,
> And find delight, writ there
> with beauty's pen.
> Examine every married lineament,
> And see how one another lends
> content:
> And what obscured in this fair
> volume lies,
> Find written in the margent of
> his eyes.
> This precious book of love, this
> unbound lover,
> To beautify him only needs a
> cover!

The other most important dramatic tradition was that of tragedy. The Elizabethan audiences liked spectacular scenes; they also had a great relish for scenes of sheer horror. This led to a school of tragic writing made popular by Kyd and Marlowe.

These plays were full of action and color and incredible wickedness, and the stage literally ran with artificial blood. Shakespeare's early tragedies are directly in this tradition, but later the convention becomes altered and improved in practice, just as that of comedy had done. The scene in *King Lear* where Gloucester has his eyes torn out stems from this convention. Lear, however, is a comparatively late play and the introduction of this scene does not distort or interrupt its organization.

Shakespeare's stylistic development falls into a quite well-defined progression. At first he wrote plays according to the habit of his rivals. He very quickly began experimenting with his technique. His main concern seems to be with tricks of language. He was finding out just what he could do. These early plays use a great deal of rhyme, seemingly just because Shakespeare liked writing rhyme. Later on, rhyme is used only when there is a quite definite dramatic purpose to justify it. Between the early plays and those which may be called mature (*The Merchant of Venice* is the first of the mature plays), there is a basic change in method. In the early works Shakespeare was taking his patterns from previous plays and writing his own pieces, quite consciously incorporating one device here and another there.

In the later period these tricks of the trade had been tested and

The world as known in 1600

Elizabethan coins

absorbed; they had become not contrived methods but part of Shakespeare's mind. This meant that, quite unconsciously, while his total attention was focused on the emotional and intellectual business of writing a masterpiece, he wrote in terms of the traditional habits he had learned and used in the earlier period. (*Henry IV, Julius Caesar, Henry V,* and *Hamlet* are the plays of this advanced stage.)

The group of plays between 1606 and 1609 shows a further new development. Having reached mastery of his medium in terms of dramatic technique (with *Othello*) and of power over the tension of thought in moving easily through scenes of comedy, pathos, and tragedy, he turned again to the actual literary quality of his plays and began to enlarge his scope quite beyond and apart from the theatrical traditions of his day. The early results of this new attempt are the two plays *King Lear* and *Macbeth*. The change in these plays is in the direction of concentration of thought. The attempt is, by using masses of images piled one on another, to convey shadings and intensities of emotion not before possible. He was trying to express the inexpressible. For example the following is from the last part of

an introduction
to Shakespeare

Lady Macbeth's famous speech in Act I, Scene v:

Come, thick night,
And pall thee in the dunnest smoke of hell,
That my keen knife see not the wound it makes,
Nor heaven peep through the blanket of the dark,
To cry, hold, hold!

Compare the concentrated imagery of this speech with Hamlet's soliloquy at the end of Act III, Scene ii.

'Tis now the very witching time of night,
When churchyards yawn, and hell itself breathes out
Contagion to this world: now could I drink hot blood,
And do such bitterness as the day
Would quake to look on.

The sentiment of these two speeches is similar, but the difference in method is striking and produces a difference again in the type of effect. The *Lear-Macbeth* type of writing produces a higher tension of subtlety but tends to collect in masses rather than to move in lines as the lighter, more transparent writing of *Hamlet* does.

Shakespeare's last plays were conceived for the new indoor theater at Blackfriars and show this is in a more sophisticated type of staging. In *The Tempest,* last and most celebrated of these late comedies, there is dancing, and much complicated staging (such as the disappearing banquet, the ship at sea, and so on). The writing of plays for the

more distinguished audience of Blackfriars, and the increased stage resources there provided, influenced the form of the plays.

The writing of these plays forms a culmination. In his early apprenticeship Shakespeare had been extravagant in word-acrobatics, testing the limits of his technique. In the Lear-Macbeth period of innovation he had tried the limits of concentrated emotion to the point almost of weakening the dramatic effectiveness of the plays. In *The Tempest* his lines are shaken out into motion again. He seems to have been able to achieve the subtlety he was after in verse of light texture and easy movement, no longer showing the tendency to heaviness or opacity visible in *King Lear* and *Macbeth*.

THE THEATER

The first public theater in London was built in the year 1576 for James Burbage and was called simply The Theatre. Before this time players' companies had performed for the public in the courtyards of the city inns. For a more select public they frequently played in the great halls of institutions, notably the Inns of Court. The stage and auditorium of the Elizabethan theater were based on these traditions and combined features of both the hall and the inn-yard. The auditorium was small. There was a pit where the orchestra seats would be in a modern playhouse; this section was for the lowest classes who stood during the performances. Around the

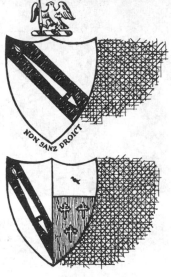

Shakespeare's Coat of Arms   Wood cut camp illustration

wall was a gallery for the gentry. The galleries and the tiring-house behind the fore-stage were roofed; the rest was open to the sky. The stage consisted of a very large platform that jutted out so that the pit audience stood on three sides of it. Behind this, under the continuation behind the stage of the gallery, was the inner stage; this was supplied with a curtain, but the open fore-stage was not. Above this inner stage was a balcony (really a continuation of the gallery), forming still another curtained stage. This gallery was used for kings addressing subjects from balconies, for the storming of walls, for Juliet's balcony and bedroom, for Cleopatra's monument and so on. Costumes and properties were extravagant (such as guillotines, fountains, ladders, etc.); extensive music was constantly used and such sound effects as cannon, drums, or unearthly screams were common; but there was no painted scenery as we know it; there was no darkness to focus attention on the stage, no facilities for stage-lighting. All these things are in marked contrast to the modern stage conventions and thus a serious problem of adaptation is posed when it comes to producing the plays under present day conditions.

The advantages are not all with the modern stage. It is true that the modern or picture stage can do more in the way of realistic effects, but this kind of realism is not important to good drama. In fact there has been a recent trend away from realistic scenery in the theater back to a conventional or stylized simplicity.

One effect of Shakespeare's stage upon his work was to make the scenes in the plays more person-scenes than place-scenes. As a matter of fact in many cases the places assigned in the texts to various scenes were not in the original and have only been added by an editor who did not understand this very fact.

It used to be said that *Antony and Cleopatra* could not be staged and was written to be read rather than acted. The grounds for this statement were that in the fourth act there were no less than fourteen scenes. To some, a scene means a change of place and requires a break in the play while scenery is shifted. To Shakespeare these scenes meant no such thing; they meant, simply, that there were fourteen different groupings of people, successively and without any break, carrying on the action of the play. The scene headings when added should have been (1) Caesar, (2) Antony and Cleopatra, (3) the common soldiers, etc., instead of (1) Before Alexandria, (2) Alexandria, a room in the palace, etc. By this you may see that with all its limitations, the Elizabethan stage had a measure of flexibility that the modern stage could envy.

Fashions in staging Shakespeare have altered radically in the last few years. At the close of the nineteenth century, Sir Herbert Beerbohm Tree staged a spectacular series of pageant productions. All the tricks of romantic realistic staging were used and, if necessary, the play was twisted, battered, and re-written to accommodate the paraphernalia.

The modern method is to produce the plays as nearly according to the text as possible and work out a compromise to achieve the sense of space and of flexibility necessary, yet without departing so far from the stage habits of today as to confuse or divert the audience. This technique was inaugurated by Granville-Barker in the early twentieth century. With the exception of such extravagant stunts as Orson Welles' production of *Julius Caesar* in modern dress (set in Chicago and complete with tommy-guns), the prevailing practice now is to use simple, stylized scenery adapted to the needs of producing the play at full length.

Much can be done in the way of learning Shakespeare through books, but the only sure way is to see a well produced performance by a good company of actors. Whatever genius Shakespeare may have possessed as a psychologist, philosopher, or poet, he was first of all a man of the theater, who knew it from the inside, and who wrote plays so well-plotted for performance that from his day up to the present, no great actor has been able to resist them.

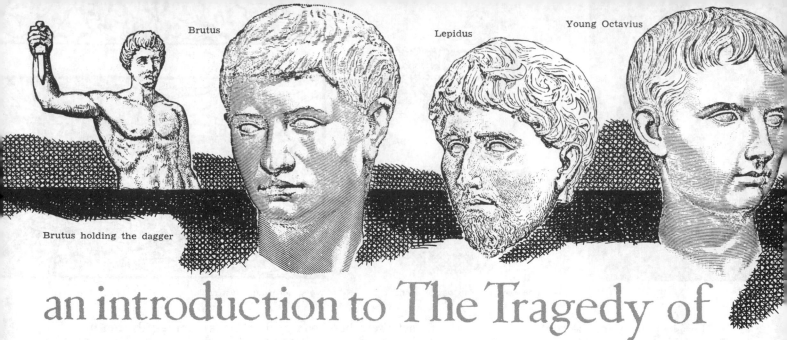

Brutus

Lepidus

Young Octavius

Brutus holding the dagger

an introduction to The Tragedy of

The play is discussed fully in the commentary that accompanies the text, and this section of the introduction is concerned only with general comment. *Julius Caesar* is the first of Shakespeare's three plays dealing with the history of Rome (the others being *Coriolanus* and *Antony and Cleopatra*) and perhaps the best preliminary to a discussion of it is to give a compressed version of the historical events on which the play is based. For the first 250 years after its founding, Rome was ruled by kings whose domination became increasingly oppressive until, in the reign of the Tarquins, the Romans revolted. This revolution was led by Lucius Junius Brutus (from whom the Brutus of our play was descended; see Cassius' reference at I,ii,159) and replaced the monarchy by a republican form of government. This government was composed of two consuls, the Roman Senate, the praetors (who administered civil justice) and the tribunes (who represented the people). Julius Caesar became a consul in 59 B.C. and both his ability and his inordinate ambition soon became apparent. He was highly successful in extending Roman power outside Italy, particularly in his Gallic campaigns, and when he returned to Italy he entered into a struggle for power with his great rival, Pompey. Caesar defeated Pompey's forces in Italy, again in Spain, and

finally and decisively in the battle of Pharsalia in Macedonia. Several other foreign campaigns followed, with Caesar making his military power absolute by defeating Pompey's sons in Spain, in 45 B.C. It was from this victory that he returned in triumph to Rome, and at this point Shakespeare's play begins. The political conflict of the play is between those who, in an attempt to preserve republican Rome, and hence their own freedom, conspire against Caesar and his drive to absolute power (Brutus, Cassius, and the other conspirators), and those who support Caesar (Antony and Octavius). The direct source for Shakespeare's play is the historian Plutarch's work, *Lives of the Noble Grecians and Romans,* in its Elizabethan translation by Sir Thomas North. This work was widely read and admired, and Shakespeare could depend on his audience, or a large part of it, being familiar with the story.

Julius Caesar was probably first produced at the Globe in 1599. At this point in his career Shakespeare had already written his history plays, dealing with the struggles for power in his own country. In them he had been concerned, not simply with historical events, but with giving dramatic form to the evils of rebellion and civil war. This was a subject of considerable contemporary importance. Queen Elizabeth's long reign was drawing to a close, there seemed no

possibility of a legitimate succession to the throne, and Elizabeth herself still refused to settle on a successor. With the certainty of hindsight we now tend to see the peaceful transition from the rule of Elizabeth to that of James I as inevitable. It was by no means inevitable to an Elizabethan of 1599, and there were ominous threats of civil disturbance and rebellion. The "domestic fury and fierce civil strife" that Antony foresees (III,i) as a result of the Brutus-Cassius rebellion would be very real to an Elizabethan audience. This is one of the major concerns of the play, and the struggle for power, and what it does to the men engaged in it, is a continuing theme in all Shakespeare's historical plays, whether the history is English or Roman.

Shakespeare begins with Plutarch's version of Roman history, but he alters it somewhat to suit his dramatic needs. The events dealt with in the play took, in fact, almost three years —from Caesar's refusal of the crown on the Feast of Lupercal in February of 44 B.C. until the second battle of Philippi in October of 42 B.C. In Shakespeare's version all this is compressed into six days. Shakespeare also subtly alters the characters he found in Plutarch.

Some commentators have felt that the play ought really to be called *The Tragedy of Marcus Brutus*. Shakespeare was to go on, after *Julius Caesar*, to the pe-

14

Antony

Julius Caesar

Julius Caesar

riod of his great tragedies (*Hamlet*, whose hero resembles Brutus in many ways, may have been his next play) and certainly Brutus has many of the characteristics of a tragic hero—a great man who, through some flaw or defect in an otherwise noble character, brings about his own destruction. Mr. John Palmer has given an admirable description of the character of Brutus. "Brutus has precisely the qualities which in every age have rendered the conscientious liberal ineffectual in public life. His convictions required him to take the lead in a political conspiracy which, for its success, called for great agility of mind, a deft and callous adjustment of means to ends, acceptance of the brutal consequences which attend an act of violence, and insight into the motives of men less scrupulous and disinterested than himself. In all these respects he was deficient. Brutus, plotting the assassination of Caesar, did violence to his character, entered into association with men whom he did not understand and involved himself in events which he was unable to control."

Brutus' nobility is everywhere in evidence. All the other characters make reference to it. "Well Brutus, thou art noble" Cassius reflects (I,ii,311). Cinna insists that the conspirators "win the noble Brutus to our party" (I,iii,141). It is clear that it is the nobility of Brutus that the conspirators want associated with their actions, and Antony's final speech sums him up as "the noblest Roman of them all" (V,v,68). His taste for music and literature, his love for Portia and hers for him, his unfailing kindness to his servants and supporters, all of this contributes to our view of Brutus as a man of courage, dignity and humanity. Yet he makes every mistake it is possible to make. He misunderstands those with whom he has to deal. The minor misjudgment of Casca leads on to the major, and fatal, misjudgment of Antony, the "masker and reveller" whom Brutus sees no need to fear. These misconceptions of character are followed by errors in action. Brutus not only allows Antony to speak at Caesar's funeral, he lets him have the important last word, trusting to Antony's promise that he will not "blame" the conspirators. He very nearly destroys his alliance with Cassius over a matter of principle. He insists on fighting a battle against Cassius' better judgment, and once committed, mistimes his attack in such a way as to jeopardize the fortunes of both his and Cassius' armies. All his failings are related, somehow, to his virtues—his idealism, innocence, and the purity of his motives. His final tragedy is twofold: it comprises both his own death and that of his wife, and the destruction (in the victory of Antony and Octavius) of the freedom and republican prin-

15

Vintage or Bacchanalian Scene

Family scene in bas-relief of marble

ciples for which he fought.

Through the first half of the play Brutus is contrasted to Cassius. Where Brutus' distrust of Caesar is a matter of principle, Cassius' hatred comes from envy and ambition. Where Brutus concerns himself with the ethical questions arising out of the conspiracy, Cassius deals with the practical matters—for example in the clever if not entirely honest way in which he plants the letters "as if they came from several citizens" urging Brutus to join the conspirators. Caesar's remarks about the "lean and hungry" Cassius who "looks quite through the deeds of men" largely determine the way we see him in the first two acts. He is acute, intelligent, and effective. Therefore when Cassius distrusts Antony, we recognize this distrust as well-founded; when he argues against allowing Antony to speak at the funeral, we know that he is right and Brutus is wrong. When, in IV,iii, he advises against Brutus' military plan, we know that that plan will bring disaster. Yet the figure of Cassius does change, or

an introduction to the tragedy of Julius Caesar

develop, in the second half of the play. In the quarrel scene (IV,iii) he bears himself with dignity, and in the reconciliation his love for Brutus is strongly emphasized. Nor do we see, in the second half, the wily conspirator of Act I. This is in part because Antony, after the funeral oration, replaces Cassius as the contrast to Brutus and the nemesis of the conspirators. Cassius' more admirable qualities are also developed toward the end of the play to add pathos to his death. Our pity for him is enhanced by the final, bitter irony that it is Cassius—the man of shrewd intelligence—who kills himself because he misunderstands the outcome of Titinius' mission.

The dramatist, unlike the novelist, does not have all the time he chooses in which to develop his characters. Therefore secondary figures are sketched briefly and simply. The presentation of Antony is relatively simple. He serves, in part, as a direct contrast to the admirable but ineffective idealism of Brutus. Brutus dismisses him as merely "gamesome," but this is another of Brutus' errors, and we know that Cassius' estimate of him as a "shrewd contriver" is the true one. We first see his brilliance in his careful handling of the conspirators after the assassination. Once he has succeeded in getting Brutus to guarantee his safety, he sets about organizing Caesar's revenge. His

funeral speech is a work of rhetorical genius, and nowhere in the play are the characters of Brutus and Antony better contrasted than in these speeches (see the commentary at III,ii). Antony's complete lack of moral scruple is further developed in IV,i. Where Brutus had spared Antony so that the conspirators would "be called purgers, not murderers," Antony, in his turn, prepares a long list of Romans to be executed. His attitude toward Lepidus ("meet to be sent on errands") illustrates his view of most men: they are, as he says, "properties" to be used.

Despite those commentators who see Caesar as a minor character in the play, his presence is felt throughout it, and most strongly after his death. Shakespeare could assume that his audience were well aware of Caesar's legendary greatness. Therefore in his presentation in the play he is able to modify and qualify this greatness somewhat. Caesar's pride is shown as being sometimes petulant, sometimes arrogant, and sometimes even stupid. Decius Brutus manipulates this pride deftly to inveigle Caesar to the Capitol on the fateful ides of March. His epilepsy, his deafness, his demagoguery and theatricality are all touched on. Shakespeare has in other plays made an ironic contrast between a king or dictator's public or official greatness, and his private weaknesses. But this is not done simply to discredit

Julius Caesar

Octavius

Roman coins

Mosaic showing
the estate
of Julius

the public figure. Shakespeare was well aware that heroes have their failings, but he was also aware that a public hero is more than just a man. He is also an idea, or a symbol, identified with the state. That is why Caesar's assassination is not only an act of murder, but also a civil disaster, with war and death as its inevitable consequence. When Brutus says, over Cassius' dead body, "O Julius Caesar thou art mighty yet!" he speaks of Caesar as a political idea rather than as a man. One of the most powerful ironies in the play lies in the fact that Brutus imagines he can "come by the spirit of Caesar" by killing him, whereas what in fact the assassination does is to give Caesar's spirit a much greater power. In this sense Caesar is the greatest force in the play, and it bears his name quite rightly.

A NOTE ON THE TEXT

Julius Caesar was first published in the First Folio of 1623. All modern versions are based on the First Folio, with minor changes (e.g., Casca for Caska, Marullus for Murellus, Murellus, etc.) and emendations. Where there are variant emendations, they are noted in the glossary. The First Folio included act divisions, but no scene divisions. The scene divisions here are those of the Globe edition, which have become standard.

17

Bibliography

EDITIONS

A New Variorum Edition of Shakespeare, ed. Horace H. Furness. New York: J. B. Lippincott, 1871——. (Reprints by The American Scholar and Dover Publications.) Each play is dealt with in a separate volume of monumental scholarship.

The Yale Shakespeare, ed. Helge Kökeritz and Charles T. Prouty. New Haven: Yale University Press, 1955——. A multi-volume edition founded on modern scholarship.

COMMENTARY AND CRITICISM

Bentley, G. E. *Shakespeare and His Theatre.* Lincoln: University of Nebraska Press, 1964 (paperback). Illuminating discussion of the actual conditions under which, and for which, Shakespeare wrote.

Bradley, A. C. *Shakespearean Tragedy: Lectures on Hamlet, Othello, King Lear, Macbeth.* New York: Macmillan, 1904. (Paperback ed.; New York: Meridian Books, 1955.) A classic examination of the great tragedies.

Chambers, Edmund K. *William Shakespeare: A Study of Facts and Problems,* 2 vols. Oxford: Clarendon Press, 1930. Indispensable source for bibliographical and historical information.

Chute, Marchette. *Shakespeare of London.* New York: E. P. Dutton, 1949. A vivid account of Shakespeare's career in the dynamic Elizabethan metropolis.

Granville-Barker, Harley. *Prefaces to Shakespeare.* London: Sidgwick & Jackson, 1927-47. (2 vols.; Princeton: Princeton University Press, 1947.) Stimulating studies of ten plays by a scholarly man of the theater.

Harbage, Alfred. *Shakespeare's Audience.* New York: Columbia University Press, 1941. Revealing approach to Shakespeare as a practical man of the theater.

Knight, Wilson. *The Wheel of Fire.* London: Oxford University Press, 1930. Stresses the power of intuition to capture the total poetic experience of Shakespeare's work.

Spurgeon, Caroline. *Shakespeare's Imagery and What It Tells Us.* Cambridge: Cambridge University Press, 1935. A psychological study of the playwright's imagery as a means to understanding the man himself.

The Tragedy
of
Julius Caesar

Dramatis Personae

JULIUS CAESAR
OCTAVIUS CAESAR
MARCUS ANTONIUS } triumvirs after the death of Julius Caesar
M. AEMILIUS LEPIDUS
CICERO
PUBLIUS } senators
POPILIUS LENA
MARCUS BRUTUS
CASSIUS
CASCA
TREBONIUS
LIGARIUS } conspirators against Julius Caesar
DECIUS BRUTUS
METELLUS CIMBER
CINNA
FLAVIUS and MARULLUS, tribunes of the people
ARTEMIDORUS, a teacher of rhetoric
A Soothsayer
CINNA, a poet
Another poet
LUCILIUS
TITINIUS
MESSALA } friends to Brutus and Cassius
YOUNG CATO
VOLUMNIUS
VARRO
CLITUS
CLAUDIUS } servants to Brutus
STRATO
LUCIUS
DARDANIUS
PINDARUS, servant to Cassius
A servant to Caesar; to Antony; to Octavius
CALPURNIA, wife to Caesar
PORTIA, wife to Brutus
The Ghost of Caesar
Senators, citizens, guards, attendants, etc.

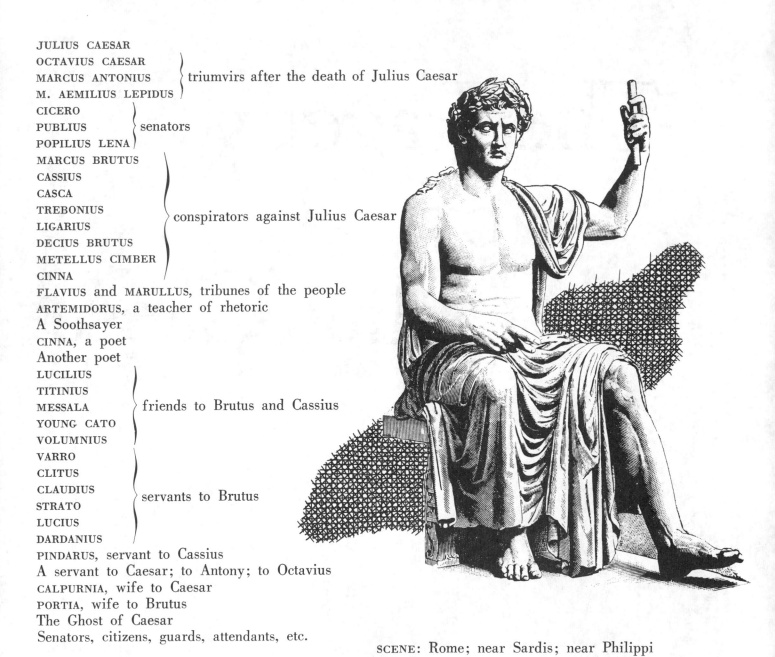

SCENE: Rome; near Sardis; near Philippi

20

JULIUS CAESAR

ACT I SCENE I

The opening scene in a Shakespearean play usually has two functions. In the first place it must make an immediate and powerful appeal to the audience's attention. This is not only good dramatic practice in general; it was especially important in the Elizabethan theater because of the informal, and sometimes boisterous, behavior of the playgoers. Here Shakespeare gets their attention (and ours) at once with Flavius' opening, angry shouts at the "commoners." Secondly, Shakespeare's first scenes often give us some suggestion of the kind of situation, or theme, which is going to develop as the play goes on. For example in HAMLET one of the main elements of the play is the dramatization of the hero's doubt and confusion, and the play opens with the tense, dramatic challenge and counter-challenge of some uneasy soldiers standing guard, suggesting to us at once that sense of confusion and uncertainty which will spread and intensify as the play continues. So here we have the two tribunes—Flavius and Marullus—who are not important as characters (they are "put to silence" in the next scene) but are dramatically significant because of what they say, both against Caesar and his plebeian admirers, introduces us to the atmosphere of strife and disunity in Rome. It is an atmosphere that is only vague and general as yet, but that will become specific as the conspiratorial designs of Cassius come to light in the next scene.

The tribunes are the official representatives of the people, and are shown here as being violently opposed to Caesar because of his attempts to obtain absolute power in Rome by becoming a king. The Roman tradition was republican—government by the senate, rather than a single authority—and it is this tradition that the tribunes here (and the Cassius-Brutus conspiracy later) are trying to uphold against the "royal" ambitions of Caesar.

All drama depends on conflict of some kind, both throughout the play as a whole, and in individual scenes; the conflict here is a verbal one, between the tribunes and the cobbler. The tribunes have authority, and their language shows it ("You blocks, you stones, you worse than senseless things!") but against this authoritarian rhetoric Shakespeare puts the verbal dexterity of the cobbler, who exasperates Flavius and Marullus by his deliberate misunderstanding of what they say, and his habit of punning, and playing on the meanings of the words he uses. When reading a Shakespeare play we

---

ACT ONE, scene one.

(ROME. A STREET)

Enter FLAVIUS, MARULLUS, *and certain commoners over the stage.* s.d.

Flavius. Hence! home, you idle creatures, get you home!
Is this a holiday? What, know you not,
Being mechanical, you ought not to walk 3
Upon a labouring day without the sign 4
Of your profession? Speak, what trade art thou? 5
    Carpenter. Why sir, a carpenter.
Marullus. Where is thy leather apron and thy rule?
What dost thou with thy best apparel on?
You, sir, what trade are you?
Cobbler. Truly sir, in respect of a fine workman, I am but, as you would say, a cobbler. 11
Marullus. But what trade art thou? Answer me directly.
Cobbler. A trade, sir, that I hope I may use with a safe conscience, which is indeed, sir, a mender of bad soles. 16
Flavius. What trade, thou knave? Thou naughty 17
knave, what trade?
Cobbler. Nay, I beseech you sir, be not out with me, 19
yet if thou be out, sir, I can mend you. 20
Marullus. What mean'st thou by that? Mend me, thou saucy fellow?
Cobbler. Why, sir, cobble you.
Flavius. Thou art a cobbler, art thou?
Cobbler. Truly sir, all that I live by is with the awl. 25
I meddle with no tradesman's matters nor women's matters, but withal—I am indeed, sir, a surgeon to old shoes. When they are in great danger, I recover 28
them. As proper men as ever trod upon neat's leather 29
have gone upon my handiwork.
Flavius. But wherefore art not in thy shop to-day?
Why dost thou lead these men about the streets?
Cobbler. Truly sir, to wear out their shoes, to get myself into more work. But indeed sir, we make holiday to see Caesar and to rejoice in his triumph. 35
Marullus. Wherefore rejoice? What conquest brings he home?
What tributaries follow him to Rome? 37
To grace in captive bonds his chariot wheels?
You blocks, you stones, you worse than senseless things!
O you hard hearts, you cruel men of Rome!
Knew you not Pompey? Many a time and oft
Have you climbed up to walls and battlements,
To towers and windows, yea, to chimney tops, 43
Your infants in your arms, and there have sat
The livelong day, with patient expectation,
To see great Pompey pass the streets of Rome.
And when you saw his chariot but appear,
Have you not made an universal shout,
That Tiber trembled underneath her banks 49

Stage Direction "over the stage": the commoners cross the stage before halting. In most productions they enter first, with Flavius and Marullus following them.

3. "Being mechanical": being artisans or workers.

4-5. "sign Of your profession": dress or symbol of your trade.

11. "cobbler": this means bungler as well as shoemaker and confuses Marullus. The cobbler puns throughout his speeches.

16. "soles": of shoes, with a pun on soul.

17. "naughty": insolent. A stronger term for the Elizabethans than for us.

19. "out": angry.

20. "out": have shoes out at the sole, or worn out.

25-28. The cobbler continues to have verbal fun at the expense of Flavius and Marullus. Here he says that he is above "meddling" with trade, or ordinary work, just as he is above pursuing women. He gives himself the grandiose title of surgeon "withal," i.e., a surgeon with an awl. In mending or re-covering shoes he makes them "recover," or heals them.

29. "neat's leather": oxhide.

35. "triumph": a triumphal procession through Rome. Caesar is returning from the defeat of Pompey's sons in Spain.

37. "tributaries": conquered rulers bringing tributes of money.

43-49. Here Shakespeare combines the London of his audience ("towers, windows, chimney tops") with the Rome of Pompey's chariot and the river Tiber.

JULIUS CAESAR

ACT I SCENE I

must always remember that the language was meant to be heard and not read, and that puns spoken from the stage are more effective than they are on the printed page. As soon as the cobbler mentions "soles" he associates the word with "souls," "with the awl" suggests "withal," and in playing on the various meanings he is able i) to get the better of his social superiors, at least for some fifteen lines, and ii) thereby give a good deal of amusement to the large element of "commoners" like himself in the Elizabethan audience. who presumably had no more love for authority than the cobbler.

Shakespeare makes another subtle but important point in the course of this scene which prepares us for a crisis later in the play. The people have come forth "to see Caesar and rejoice in his triumph" in the traditional procession through the streets in honor of a returning hero. But Marullus points out how fickle their admiration is, for in the same manner they had once welcomed Pompey with "an universal shout," just as they now welcome the man "who comes in triumph over Pompey's blood." On the stage before us the holiday mood of the crowd changes at once; they are "moved" Flavius says, "and vanish tongue-tied in their guiltiness." Shakespeare impresses on us the way in which the crowd can be swayed since he wants us to recall it later in the play, at the climax of III,iii, when Antony's speech converts the same crowd from the conspirators' cause to his own.

ACT I SCENE II

We ought to recall at this juncture betwen scenes one and two, and indeed at every change of scene, that Shakespeare wrote for a theater which had nothing like our prolonged scene-changes, involving the lowering of a curtain and the changing of stage props and furnishings. On the Elizabethan stage one scene ran directly into another, giving an effect rather like that of a moving picture dissolving from one shot to the next. The importance of this lies in the fact that Shakespeare often used the ending of one scene as a comment on, or introduction to the next. Here, for example, Flavius and Marullus leave the stage at one side, talking of the man who would "keep us all in servile fearfulness" and immediately the object of their fear, Caesar himself, enters at the other side. Scene i had also prepared us for Scene ii by giving us a general impression of fear and discord: now that impression will gain sharper focus through the delineation of the principal char-

---

To hear the replication of your sounds 50
Made in her concave shores? 51
And do you now put-on your best attire?
And do you now cull out a holiday? 53
And do you now strew flowers in his way
That comes in triumph over Pompey's blood? 55
Be gone!
Run to your houses, fall upon your knees,
Pray to the gods to intermit the plague 58
That needs must light on this ingratitude.
 Flavius. Go, go, good countrymen, and for this fault
Assemble all the poor men of your sort;
Draw them to Tiber banks, and weep your tears
Into the channel, till the lowest stream
Do kiss the most exalted shores of all. 64
     [*Exeunt the* commoners.
See, whe'r their basest mettle be not moved. 65
They vanish tongue-tied in their guiltiness.
Go you down that way towards the Capitol; 67
This way will I. Disrobe the images 68
If you do find them decked with ceremonies. 69
 Marullus. May we do so?
You know it is the feast of Lupercal. 71
 Flavius. It is no matter. Let no images
Be hung with Caesar's trophies. I'll about
And drive away the vulgar from the streets. 74
So do you too, where you perceive them thick.
These growing feathers, plucked from Caesar's wing 76
Will make him fly an ordinary pitch,
Who else would soar above the view of men
And keep us all in servile fearfulness 79
       [*Exeunt.*

Scene two.

(Rome. A Public Place.)

Flourish. Enter CAESAR, ANTONY *(for the course),* CAL-PURNIA, PORTIA, DECIUS, CICERO, BRUTUS, CASSIUS, CASCA, *a great crowd following, among them a Soothsayer; after them,* MARULLUS *and* FLAVIUS. s.d.
 Caesar. Calpurnia.
 Casca.   Peace, ho! Caesar speaks.
 Caesar.   Calpurnia.
 Calpurnia. Here, my lord.
 Caesar. Stand you directly in Antonius' way 3
When he doth run his course. Antonius.
 Antony. Caesar, my lord?
 Caesar. Forget not in your speed, Antonius,
To touch Calpurnia; for our elders say
The barren, touched in this holy chase,
Shake off their sterile curse.
 Antony.   I shall remember
When Caesar says 'Do this,' it is performed.
 Caesar. Set on, and leave no ceremony out.
          [*Flourish.*
 Soothsayer. Caesar!
 Caesar. Ha! Who calls?

22

---

50. "replication": echo, reverberation.

51. "concave shores": overhanging banks.

53. "cull out": choose to take. This is meant ironically, since the artisans could not choose their own holidays.

55. "Pompey's blood": the blood of Pompey's sons and his armies.

58. "intermit": hold off.

64. "most exalted shores": highest banks.

65. "whe'r": frequent in Shakespeare for whether.
"mettle": temperament, disposition.
"moved": affected, changed—i.e., to guilt at forgetting Pompey.

67. "Capitol": the Temple of Jupiter on the Capitoline Hill where the state business of Rome was transacted.

68. "images": statues.
69. "ceremonies": ornaments such as garlands or wreaths.

71. "Lupercal": the Lupercalia, festival of the god Lupercus.

74. "the vulgar": the common people.

76-79. The image is from falconry, with Caesar as the falcon whose "wing" (power) will be weaker if his "growing feathers" (popular support) are plucked, causing him to fly at a lower "pitch" (height).

Stage Direction "Flourish": an extended sounding of trumpets, used on the Elizabethan stage to announce the entrance of a procession, or of a ruler and his court. A "sennet" (l. 24) was a briefer version.

Stage Direction "for the course": stripped for running.

3. "Antonius": Shakespeare occasionally alters the form of names to maintain the rhythm of the iambic pentametre verse. Here he needs an extra syllable, but compare l. 204, below.

JULIUS CAESAR

ACT I SCENE II

acters—particularly Caesar, Cassius and Brutus.

This is Caesar's first appearance on the stage, but we must remember that the Elizabethan audience were familiar with his story, and that Shakespeare takes this familiarity into account and uses it. The Elizabethans were fascinated by Roman history, perhaps because they were themselves at this point creating an empire, and saw Rome both as a precedent and an analogy. For them Caesar was, by definition, a monumental figure, "the foremost man of all this world" as Brutus calls him later in the play (IV,iii,22). Therefore Shakespeare did not have the task (as a modern playwright might have) of establishing Caesar's greatness. Assuming that his audience takes Caesar's stature for granted, he can go on to qualify and re-define the character for his own purposes in the play. Furthermore to enlarge on the legendary Caesar—the hero and saviour of Rome, pure and simple —would necessarily make the conspiracy against him a matter of irresponsible jealousy and viciousness. The conspirators must have some reason on their side, and we already know from Scene i that Caesar threatens both the liberty of the Roman citizens and the laws of the republic with his dictatorial designs. Now we are shown a Caesar in whom Shakespeare reveals, in one or two subtle details, the weakness that may accompany the will to dominate.

At one word from Caesar the crowd is silenced by Casca, and Calpurnia and Antony are ordered to step forward. Caesar's authority is clear, it is asserted at once, and underlined by Antony's "When Caesar says 'Do this,' it is performed." We may recall at this point the introduction of another Shakespearean ruler, who will also be murdered by his subject. But in MACBETH Duncan, the king, is deliberately made an example of both justice and gentleness in order to emphasize the enormity of Macbeth's crime. Caesar, on the other hand, is consciously arrogant; one feels, in what he says, his sense of being set apart from and above other men. Later on in this scene (ll. 199 ff.) he announces that, as Caesar, he is not "liable to fear" as others are: "I rather tell thee what is to be feared/Than what I fear, for always I am Caesar." Here he disregards the Soothsayer ("He is a dreamer") who warns him of the ides of March. It is worth noting here that prophesies of this kind occur in several of Shakespeare's plays, always with the same dramatic function: dreams, omens, auguries, and indeed any sort of supernatural prediction are power-

---

Casca. Bid every noise be still. Peace yet again!

Caesar. Who is it in the press that calls on me? 15
I hear a tongue shriller than all the music
Cry 'Caesar!' Speak. Caesar is turned to hear.

Soothsayer. Beware the ides of March. 18

Caesar.   What man is that?

Brutus. A soothsayer bids you beware the ides of
    March.

Caesar. Set him before me; let me see his face.

Cassius. Fellow, come from the throng; look upon
    Caesar.

Caesar. What say'st thou to me now? Speak once
    again.

Soothsayer. Beware the ides of March.

Caesar. He is a dreamer. Let us leave him. Pass.
    [*Sennet. Exeunt all except* BRUTUS *and* CASSIUS.

Cassius. Will you go see the order of the course? 25

Brutus. Not I.

Cassius. I pray you do.

Brutus. I am not gamesome. I do lack some part 28
Of that quick spirit that is in Antony. 29
Let me not hinder, Cassius, your desires.
I'll leave you.

Cassius. Brutus, I do observe you now of late;
I have not from your eyes that gentleness 33
And show of love as I was wont to have.
You bear too stubborn and too strange a hand 35
Over your friend that loves you. 36

Brutus.   Cassius,
Be not deceived. If I have veiled my look, 37
I turn the trouble of my countenance
Merely upon myself. Vexed I am 39
Of late with passions of some difference, 40
Conceptions only proper to myself, 41
Which give some soil, perhaps, to my behaviours; 42
But let not therefore my good friends be grieved
(Among which number, Cassius, be you one)
Nor construe any further my neglect 45
Than that poor Brutus, with himself at war,
Forgets the shows of love to other men.

Cassius. Then, Brutus, I have much mistook your 48
    passion;
By means whereof this breast of mine hath buried 49
Thoughts of great value, worthy cogitations.
Tell me, good Brutus, can you see your face?

Brutus. No, Cassius; for the eye sees not itself
But by reflection, by some other things.

Cassius. 'Tis just.
And it is very much lamented, Brutus,
That you have no such mirrors as will turn
Your hidden worthiness into your eye,
That you might see your shadow. I have heard
Where many of the best respect in Rome, 59
(Except immortal Caesar), speaking of Brutus, 60
And groaning underneath this age's yoke,
Have wished that noble Brutus had his eyes. 62

Brutus. Into what dangers would you lead me,
    Cassius,
That you would have me seek into myself
For that which is not in me?

15. "press": crowd.

18. "ides": the fifteenth day of the month.

25. "order": sequence of events.

28. "gamesome": sportive.

29. "quick": light, lively. The evidence that Brutus is troubled by Caesar's threat to republican freedom appears early in the scene and Cassius is quick to note it.

33. "I . . . eyes": i.e., I do not see in your eyes.

35-6. "You . . . friend": the metaphor is from riding. Cassius says that Brutus handles him too roughly.

37-39. "If . . . myself": i.e., if I have seemed unfriendly it is because I am concerned with my own thoughts.

39. "Merely": wholly.

40. "passions . . . difference": conflicting emotions.

41. "proper": belonging.

42. "soil": blemish.

45. "construe": understand (with the accent on the first syllable).

48. "passion": emotion.

49. "By . . . buried": i.e., I have therefore concealed.

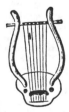

59. "best respect": highest reputation.

60. "(Except immortal Caesar)": spoken with quiet irony; Cassius begins to be specific about what he thinks is amiss in Rome.

62. "Brutus . . . eyes": i.e., that Brutus saw where he himself stood.

ACT I SCENE II

ful devices for setting up a sense of dramatic anticipation in the audience—usually of some ominous or catastrophic event. Caesar's pride in disregarding any sort of warning or advice (here and in II,ii,1 ff.) is itself, we realize, an element in his downfall.

It is also significant that the Soothsayer's warning is actually given to Caesar by Brutus. This is one example of the various kinds of dramatic irony that Shakespeare uses continually in his plays. Sometimes the irony is conscious (as when Cassius, l. 60, refers to "immortal Caesar" at the time when he is in fact planning Caesar's "mortality," or death) or the irony may be unconscious—i.e., understood in an ordinary sense by the characters on the stage, but in a further, ironic sense by us. Here, the friend who warns Caesar will become his assassin, as everyone in the audience knows. This is a minor example of dramatic irony, but Shakespeare was attentive to such details; there are more, and larger, examples of this kind of irony later in the play.

Most of the scene is given to the dialogue between Cassius and Brutus, and these two major characters are carefully introduced and developed. Brutus' very first line (19) is, as we have seen, an ironic touch. It is also a line that (as the critic-director Sir Harley Granville-Barker has pointed out) gives us something of the quality of Brutus himself: it is "measured, dispassionate, tinged with disdain." This quality—aloof, thoughtful, and perhaps a little cold—is expanded in Brutus' next lines (28-31). He is not "gamesome," nor does he have the "quick spirit" of Antony, and his first act is to attempt to leave the stage, when he is detained by Cassius.

The debate between Cassius and Brutus begins with Brutus' admission that he is "with himself at war," thereby giving Cassius his opportunity. From this point to line 161 he does almost all the talking, and these hundred-odd lines are a masterful piece of insinuation and persuasion. Cassius goes to work cautiously, beginning with praise of Brutus' "hidden worthiness," and the respect the rest of Rome has for him. At one point in the passage (ll. 60-64) Cassius pauses ironically on Caesar's "immortal," or godlike, quality; but he is too careful to enlarge on the subject until Brutus himself brings it up, and this happens at line 79, with the offstage shout from the crowd. These two shouts are carefully placed in the development of the argument: they both bring forth almost involuntary responses from Brutus that show us

Cassius. Therefore, good Brutus, be prepared to hear;
And since you know you cannot see yourself
So well as by reflection, I, your glass, 68
Will modestly discover to yourself 69
That of yourself which you yet know not of.
And be not jealous on me, gentle Brutus. 71
Were I a common laughter, or did use 72
To stale with ordinary oaths my love 73
To every new protester; if you know 74
That I do fawn on men and hug them hard,
And after scandal them; or if you know 76
That I profess myself in banqueting 77
To all the rout, then hold me dangerous. 78
       Flourish and shout. s.d.
Brutus. What means this shouting? I do fear the people
Choose Caesar for their king.
Cassius.   Ay, do you fear it?
Then must I think you would not have it so.
Brutus. I would not Cassius; yet I love him well.
But wherefore do you hold me here so long?
What is it that you would impart to me?
If it be aught toward the general good,
Set honour in one eye and death i' th' other,
And I will look on both indifferently; 87
For let the gods so speed me as I love 88
The name of honour more than I fear death.
Cassius. I know that virtue to be in you, Brutus,
As well as I do know your outward favour.
Well, honour is the subject of my story.
I cannot tell what you and other men
Think of this life; but for my single self,
I had as lief not be as live to be
In awe of such a thing as I myself. 96
I was borne free as Caesar; so were you.
We both have fed as well, and we can both
Endure the winter's cold as well as he.
For once, upon a raw and gusty day,
The troubled Tiber chafing with her shores, 101
Caesar said to me, 'Dar'st thou, Cassius, now
Leap in with me into this angry flood
And swim to yonder point?' Upon the word,
Accoutred as I was, I plunged in 105
And bade him follow. So indeed he did.
The torrent roared, and we did buffet it
With lusty sinews, throwing it aside
And stemming it with hearts of controversy. 109
But ere we could arrive the point proposed,
Caesar cried, 'Help me Cassius, or I sink!'
I, as Aeneas, our great ancestor, 112
Did from the flames of Troy upon his shoulder
The old Anchises bear, so from the waves of Tiber
Did I the tired Caesar. And this man
Is now become a god, and Cassius is
A wretched creature and must bend his body 117
If Caesar carelessly but nod on him.
He had a fever when he was in Spain,
And when the fit was on him, I did mark
How he did shake. 'Tis true, this god did shake.
His coward lips did from their colour fly,

68. "glass": mirror.

69. "modestly": without exaggeration.

71. "jealous": suspicious.

72. "laughter": object of laughter or ridicule. Some editors print "laugher".

73. "stale": cheapen. "ordinary": a tavern.

74. "new protester": i.e., every newcomer who declares his friendship.

76. "scandal": slander.

77-78. "profess . . . rout": proclaim my friendship to everyone ("all the rout") while celebrating.

78. "dangerous": unreliable, unable to keep secrets.

Stage Direction "shout": here and at l. 132 dramatically reminds Brutus and Cassius (and the audience) of Caesar's popularity with the mob.

87. "indifferently": impartially, with equal favor.

88. "so . . . as": assist me because.

96. "such . . . myself": i.e., another man like myself, in this case Caesar.

101. "chafing with": beating on.

105. "accoutred": in armor.

109. "hearts of controversy": in rivalry.

112. Cassius' reference to Aeneas, the founder of Rome, is intended to remind Brutus of Rome's great heritage now threatened by Caesar's ambition.

117. "bend": bow in reverence.

JULIUS CAESAR

ACT I SCENE II

that he, too, has Caesar and his ambition in mind. To Brutus' first reaction—"I do fear the people/ Choose Caesar for their king"— Cassius replies with great care— "Then must I think you would not have it so." It is important for his purpose to make Brutus, rather than himself, the one who first suggests the danger of Caesar. He succeeds in this, but is too clever to press the point home. Instead he takes up a phrase used by Brutus—"the name of honour"—and moves toward his subject from another direction. Brutus has said that the notion of honor is close to his heart, and Cassius next associates honour with the idea of freedom, and specifically with freedom from Caesar (ll. 95-97). The story of Cassius' rescue of Caesar from the Tiber follows, and in it two points are made. The first (and most obvious) is the reduction of Caesar from godlike superiority to human frailty (one imagines Cassius' disdain at l. 121: " 'Tis true, this GOD did shake!"). The second point lies in Cassius' reminder to Brutus, through the figure of Aeneas "our great ancestor," of the founding of Rome, and the whole Roman heritage. For Brutus this means the tradition of republican freedom, and Cassius reminds him later of the fact that his own forbears had defended this freedom against the royalist Tarquins (l. 159). Throughout his account of the Tiber incident, Cassius increases the force and overt bitterness of his denunciation until, at Brutus' reaction to the second offstage shout (l. 132), his voice rises to the fury of "Shy man, he doth bestride the narrow world/ Like a Colossus..."

Notice that once Cassius has attacked Caesar directly, the whole tone of his argument changes. At the outset he spoke vaguely of his own "worthy cogitations" and asserted that "honour is the subject of my story"; his appeal was to Brutus' general sense of right and wrong. But once he is assured that Brutus will listen to him, his appeals to justice and morality are increasingly accompanied by personal venom and envy. The great Caesar is "of feeble temper," "a sick girl," while he and Brutus "peep about/To find ourselves dishonourable graves." We already know the ambition of Caesar, the man in power. In some of Cassius' speeches we begin to see the ambition of the man excluded from power, with its sour frustration: "The fault, dear Brutus, is not in our stars/But in ourselves, that we are underlings."

Brutus' attitude throughout all this has been non-committal. He is at first puzzled by Cassius ("What is it that you would impart to me?"), and it is part of the pur-

And that same eye whose bend doth awe the world
Did lose his lustre. I did hear him groan.
Ay, and that tongue of his that bade the Romans
Mark him and write his speeches in their books,
'Alas,' it cried, 'give me some drink, Titinius,'
As a sick girl! Ye gods, it doth amaze me
A man of such a feeble temper should
So get the start of the majestic world   130
And bear the palm alone.

Shout. Flourish.

Brutus. Another general shout?
I do believe that these applauses are
For some new honours that are heaped on Caesar.
Cassius. Why, man, he doth bestride the narrow
    world
Like a Colossus, and we petty men   136
Walk under his huge legs and peep about
To find ourselves dishonourable graves.
Men at some time are masters of their fates.
The fault, dear Brutus, is not in our stars,
But in ourselves, that we are underlings.
'Brutus,' and 'Caesar.' What should be in that
    'Caesar'?
Why should that name be sounded more than yours? 143
Write them together: yours is as fair a name.
Sound them: it doth become the mouth as well.
Weigh them: It is as heavy. Conjure with 'em:
'Brutus' will start a spirit as soon as 'Caesar.'   147
Now in the names of all the gods at once,
Upon what meat doth this our Caesar feed
That he is grown so great? Age thou art shamed.
Rome, thou hast lost the breed of noble bloods.
When went there by an age since the great Flood   152
But it was famed with more than with one man?   153
When could they say (till now) that talked of Rome
That her wide walks encompassed but one man?   155
Now is it Rome indeed, and room enough,   156
When there is in it but one only man.
O, you and I have heard our fathers say
There was a Brutus once that would have brooked   159
Th' eternal devil to keep his state in Rome
As easily as a king.   161
Brutus. That you do love me I am nothing jealous.   162
What you would work me to, I have some aim.
How I have thought of this, and of these times,
I shall recount hereafter. For this present,
I would not so (with love I might entreat you)   166
Be any further moved. What you have said
I will consider; what you have to say
I will with patience hear, and find a time
Both meet to hear and answer such high things.   170
Till then, my noble friend, chew upon this:
Brutus had rather be a villager
Than to repute himself a son of Rome
Under these hard conditions as this time
Is like to lay upon us.
Cassius.   I am glad
That my weak words have struck but thus much
    show
Of fire from Brutus.

Enter CAESAR *and his train.*   s.d.

130. "get the start": i.e., a head start; the metaphor from the running of a race is carried on in the victor's "palm" in the next line.

136. "Colossus": the huge statue of Apollo at the harbour of Rhodes. It was erroneously thought that its legs spanned the harbour entrance.

143. "sounded": proclaimed.

147. "start": invoke, as in a prayer to a god.

152. "great Flood": the classical or pagan version of Noah's Flood.

153. "But . . . man": i.e., has there ever been another age in which a single man has been in this position?

155. "walks": public parks and gardens that have become (Cassius suggests) Caesar's private preserve.

156. "Rome . . . room": these words were pronounced alike by the Elizabethans, and Cassius' pun is meant to suggest that all of Rome is now the single "room" of one man.

159. "a Brutus once": an ancestor of Brutus, Lucius Junius Brutus, who helped establish the Roman republic by driving out the Tarquins.

159-61. i.e., would no more have permitted a king in Rome than a devil.

162. "nothing jealous": have no doubt. The Elizabethans frequently used "jealous" in the sense of suspicious.

166. "so": in this manner.

170. "meet": proper.

Stage Direction "train": followers.

pose of the scene to indicate Brutus' simplicity in matters of political intrigue. The very manner in which Cassius develops his argument is that of a practiced manipulator working on an innocent subject. We are by no means certain just how far Brutus has understood Cassius, and it is part of Shakespeare's design to keep us uncertain: Brutus would not be Brutus if he realized Cassius' plan at once and fell in with it. The speech in answer to Cassius beginning at line 164 does not seem to tell us much: Brutus shares "some aim" with Cassius, but does not wish "to be any further moved." The content of the speech is vague and ambiguous, but Shakespeare often tells us much about a character through the form, or manner in which he speaks. Here the phrases and sentences are brief, the rhythms short and choppy, all suggesting tight, controlled, difficult speech. Compare the confident, impassioned rhythms of Cassius, and his long, powerful phrases. Brutus' language and delivery are those of a man laboring in the uncertainty of a powerful conflict. He ends with the uneasy and inconclusive assertion that "no son of Rome" should accept the "hard conditions" of the time.

Caesar's party returns to the stage, and Caesar's remarks concerning Cassius confirm much of what we had inferred from the earlier dialogue. The "lean and hungry look" is an implicit direction from Shakespeare as to how the actor should play the role. The cleverness that Caesar notes in Cassius where human actions and motives are concerned ("he looks/Quite through the deeds of men") is clear to us after hearing his analysis of Caesar himself, and watching his artful handling of Brutus. Finally it is, of course, ironic that it is Caesar himself who sees the threat of Cassius most clearly: "such men are dangerous." Yet Caesar's own pride, given aggressive expression in his next speech (ll. 198-214) makes it impossible for him to see the danger he is in.

Casca is drawn aside by Brutus and Cassius to report to them (and to us) what has been happening offstage. Casca speaks in prose for two reasons: i) he is described as "sour" and "blunt," and represents a fairly common type on the Elizabethan stage—the cynical realist with harsh speech and an abrasive manner—who is suited better to prose than to more polished and formal blank verse, and ii) the rhythms of iambic pentametre, or blank verse, despite Shakespeare's flexible and

Brutus. The games are done, and Caesar is returning.

Cassius. As they pass by, pluck Casca by the sleeve,
And he will (after his sour fashion) tell you
What hath proceeded worthy note to-day.

Brutus. I will do so. But look you, Cassius,
The angry spot doth glow on Caesar's brow,
And all the rest look like a chidden train.
Calpurnia's cheek is pale, and Cicero
Looks with such ferret and such fiery eyes
As we have seen him in the Capitol,
Being crossed in conference by some senators. 188

Cassius. Casca will tell us what the matter is.

Caesar. Antonius.

Antony. Caesar?

Caesar. Let me have men about me that are fat, 192
Sleek-headed men, and such as sleep a-nights.
Yond Cassius has a lean and hungry look. 194
He thinks too much. Such men are dangerous.

Antony. Fear him not Caesar; he's not dangerous.
He is a noble Roman, and well given. 197

Caesar. Would he were fatter! But I fear him not.
Yet if my name were liable to fear, 199
I do not know the man I should avoid
So soon as that spare Cassius. He reads much,
He is a great observer, and he looks
Quite through the deeds of men. He loves no plays 203
As thou dost, Antony; he hears no music. 204
Seldom he smiles, and smiles in such a sort 205
As if he mocked himself and scorned his spirit
That could be moved to smile at anything.
Such men as he be never at heart's ease
Whiles they behold a greater than themselves,
And therefore are they very dangerous.
I rather tell thee what is to be feared
Than what I fear; for always I am Caesar.
Come on my right hand, for this ear is deaf,
And tell me truly what thou think'st of him.

[*Sennet. Exeunt* CAESAR *and his train.*
CASCA *remains.*

Casca. You pulled me by the cloak. Would you speak with me?

Brutus. Ay, Casca. Tell us what hath chanced to-day
That Caesar looks so sad. 217

Casca. Why, you were with him, were you not?

Brutus. I should not then ask Casca what had chanced.

Casca. Why, there was a crown offered him; and being offered him, he put it by the back of his hand thus; and then the people fell a-shouting.

Brutus. What was the second noise for?

Casca. Why, for that too.

Cassius. They shouted thrice. What was the last cry for?

Casca. Why, for that too.

Brutus. Was the crown offered him thrice?

Casca. Ay, marry was't! and he put it by thrice, 229
every time gentler than other; and at every putting-by mine honest neighbours shouted.

Cassius. Who offered him the crown?

Casca. Why, Antony.

Brutus. Tell us the manner of it, gentle Casca. 234

188. "crossed": opposed.

192-94. Caesar's distinction between "fat" and "lean" repeats the ancient proverbial notion of "fat" as amiable and satisfied, "lean" as dissatisfied and envious.

197. "well given": well disposed.

199. "Yet . . . fear": if I were capable of being afraid.

203. "Quite . . . men": i.e., through their actions and into their motives.

204. "music": dislike of music in Shakespeare's plays and for the Elizabethans generally represented a defect, or disharmony of character. In THE MERCHANT OF VENICE Lorenzo says
> That man that has no music in himself
> Nor is not moved with concord of sweet sounds
> Is fit for treasons...
and note later in the play Brutus' fondness for music (IV,iii).

205. "sort": way.

217. "sad": troubled.

229. "marry": an oath, by (the Virgin) Mary!

234. "gentle": used here in two senses, i) noble, or well-born, and ii) mild or amiable (ironic when applied to the "sour" Casca).

JULIUS CAESAR

ACT I SCENE II

varied handling of it, can develop a certain monotony over long periods on the stage, and we have just had more than two hundred lines of it. The prose of the next sixty lines gives us a rhythmic change of pace.

In making Casca a rough-tongued cynic, Shakespeare departs from his source in Plutarch and he does so in order to give us, through Casca, a cynical and disillusioned view of Caesar. In Casca's report, Caesar is a demogogue. Offered a crown, Caesar "would fain have had it" until he sensed the people's displeasure, at which point he made the dramatic gesture described in lines 257-58, apparently with such a show of sincerity that had Casca been an ordinary member of the crown "I would I might go to hell" rather than have disbelieved him. Casca's reference to the "tag-rag people" clapping as though they were in a theater is a significant underlining of an impression we get throughout: Caesar regarding himself as an heroic actor, and playing to an audience. Casca is equally hard on the people themselves. If Caesar is a fake, then they are dupes, and his contempt is summed up in the lines describing the girls who hear Caesar's apology and "cried 'Alas, good soul!' and forgave him with all their hearts. But there's no heed to be taken of them. If Caesar had stabbed their mothers, they would have done no less." It is an unflattering portrait of a mob, but necessary to Shakespeare's purposes later in III,ii and iii, where both the mob's pliancy and its brutality play an important part. At the end of his account Casca adds, off-handedly, a last detail, and it is the more powerful for being off-handed. Marullus and Flavius, Casca says, "for pulling scarfs off Caesar's images, are put to silence." Having seen Caesar the demagogue, we are reminded again of the efficient brutality with which his regime operates.

Shakespeare builds his characters and develops his themes in careful, subtle touches, and we notice one here, after Casca leaves. Brutus remarks on the way Casca has changed since his youth. Where he was once "quick" he is now "blunt." But Cassius at once points out that this is only a "form" or pretence—which Cassius sees through—and we recall Caesar's remark about Cassius' ability to "look quite through the deeds of men." In contrast to Brutus (and they are contrasted throughout the first half of the play), Cassius is the astute judge of men and situations. It will be he who sees the threat of Antony, and the danger of letting him live to speak at

Casca. I can as well be hanged as tell the manner of it. It was mere foolery; I did not mark it. I saw Mark Antony offer him a crown—yet 'twas not a crown neither, 'twas one of these coronets—and, as 238 I told you, he put it by once; but for all that, to my thinking, he would fain have had it. Then he offered it to him again; then he put it by again; but to my thinking, he was very loath to lay his fingers off it. And then he offered it the third time. He put it the third time by; and still as he refused it, the rabble-ment hooted, and clapped their chopt hands, and 245 threw up their sweaty nightcaps, and uttered such a deal of stinking breath because Caesar refused the crown that it had almost choked Caesar; for he swounded and fell down at it. And for mine own 249 part, I durst not laugh, for fear of opening my lips and receiving the bad air.

Cassius. But soft, I pray you. What, did Caesar 252 swound?

Casca. He fell down in the market place and foamed at the mouth and was speechless.

Brutus. 'Tis very like; he hath the falling sickness. 256

Cassius. No, Caesar hath it not; but you and I, And honest Casca, we have the falling sickness.

Casca. I know not what you mean by that, but I am sure Caesar fell down. If the rag-tag people did 260 not clap him and hiss him, according as he pleased and displeased them, as they use to do the players in the theatre, I am no true man.

Brutus. What said he when he came unto himself?

Casca. Marry, before he fell down, when he perceived the common herd was glad he refused the crown, he plucked me ope his doublet and offered 267 them his throat to cut. An I had been a man of any occupation, if I would not have taken him at a word, 269 I would I might go to hell among the rogues. And so he fell. When he came to himself again, he said, if he had done or said anything amiss, he desired their worships to think it was his infirmity. Three or four wenches where I stood cried 'Alas, good soul!' and forgave him with all their hearts. But there's no heed to be taken of them. If Caesar had stabbed their mothers, they would have done no less.

Brutus. And after that, he came thus sad away?

Casca. Ay.

Cassius. Did Cicero say anything?

Casca. Ay, he spoke Greek.

Cassius. To what effect?

Casca. Nay, an I tell you that, I'll ne'er look you i' the face again. But those that understood him smiled at one another and shook their heads; but for mine own part, it was Greek to me. I could tell 286 you more news too. Marullus and Flavius, for pulling scarfs off Caesar's images, are put to silence. 288 Fare you well. There was more foolery yet, if I could remember it.

Cassius. Will you sup with me to-night, Casca?

Casca. No, I am promised forth.

Cassius. Will you dine with me to-morrow?

Casca. Ay, if I be alive, and your mind hold, and 294 your dinner worth eating.

238. "coronets": small crown, or perhaps a laurel wreath.

245. "chopt": chapped.

249. "swounded": fainted.

252. "But soft": slowly.

256. "falling sickness": Brutus refers to Caesar's epilepsy. Cassius is quick to take up the phrase and give it another meaning. They are "falling" through Caesar's rise.

260. "rag-tag": ragged.

267. "plucked me ope": opened. Caesar wants to assure the crowd of his sincerity.

269. "occupation": working man.

286. "Greek to me": in fact Plutarch says specifically that Casca could speak Greek. In this phrase (which has become a part of the language) Shakespeare makes Casca disclaim any knowledge that might make him appear sophisticated or polished. He maintains his rough-hewn "blunt" and "sour" character. See Brutus' and Cassius' comments at l. 298 ff. below.

288. "put to silence": a euphemism for executed.

294. "your mind hold": i) if you don't change your mind, ii) if you are still sane.

ACT I SCENE II

Caesar's funeral. It is Cassius who is the practical mind of the conspiracy, and Brutus who, though he brings to it all his integrity, perhaps does not fully understand its working.

Brutus leaves, and Cassius speaks the soliloquy which closes the scene, and is the first soliloquy of the play. The soliloquy—in which the actor, alone on the stage, speaks his thought directly to the audience—was one of the most useful devices of the Elizabethan theater, and one which modern realistic playwrights badly miss. The soliloquy could do several things. It might give us a new insight to the character who speaks it, or provide a general comment on the progress of the action. Cassius' soliloquy does both these things. Certainly he reveals a good deal about himself: here he is a vindictive and cold-blooded schemer (see glossary, I. 318). In part, his villainy here gives dramatic impetus to the movement of the play; the audience wants to see just how it will issue into action. The Cassius of the scenes to come is never quite as Machiavellian as this again. The soliloquy also serves to prepare us directly for the organization of the conspiracy, and it ends with a ringing prediction of the troubles to come. When we recall the almost instantaneous scene-changes in the Elizabethan theater, we realize that the "thunder" which introduces scene three will begin to roll, with ominous effect, on Cassius' final words "...or worse days endure."

ACT I SCENE III

Scene three gives us one of the many examples of the way in which Shakespeare compresses historical or chronological time as he sees fit, in order to give us—what is far more important on the stage—a sense of dramatic continuity. Historically the Feast of Lupercal and the eve of the ides of March (respectively Scenes ii and iii of this act) were separated by about a month. But Shakespeare's dramatic imagination runs them together so that the "worse days" that Cassius predicts are with us immediately, in the "thunder and lightning" of the opening of Scene iii.

Readers of Shakespeare may wonder why, since he wrote for an open theater in which performances were given in the afternoon, he wrote so many nocturnal scenes. But neither Shakespeare nor his audience worried about the sort of realistic imitation of night that the theatrical electricians can produce on our stage. Shakespeare creates night, as he creates so many other things on his stage, through language; and he can

---

Cassius. Good. I will expect you.
Casca. Do so. Farewell both.　　　　　　　[*Exit.*
Brutus. What a blunt fellow is this grown to be!
He was quick mettle when he went to school.　299
Cassius. So is he now in execution
Of any bold or noble enterprise,
However he puts on this tardy form.　　　302
This rudeness is a sauce to his good wit,
Which gives men stomach to digest his words
With better appetite.
Brutus. And so it is. For this time I will leave you.
To-morrow, if you please to speak with me,
I will come home to you; or if you will,
Come home to me, and I will wait for you.
Cassius. I will do so. Till then, think of the world.　310
　　　　　　　　　　　　　　　[*Exit* BRUTUS.

Well, Brutus, thou art noble; yet I see
Thy honourable mettle may be wrought　312
From that it is disposed. Therefore it is meet　313
That noble minds keep ever with their likes;　314
For who so firm that cannot be seduced?
Caesar doth bear me hard; but he loves Brutus.　316
If I were Brutus now and he were Cassius,
He should not humour me. I will this night,　318
In several hands, in at his windows throw,　319
As if they came from several citizens,
Writings, all tending to the great opinion　321
That Rome holds of his name; wherein obscurely　322
Caesar's ambition shall be glanced at.　323
And after this let Caesar seat him sure,
For we will shake him, or worse days endure. [*Exit.*

Scene three.

(ROME. A STREET.)

Thunder and lightning. Enter, from opposite sides, s.d.
CASCA *with his sword drawn, and* CICERO.

Cicero. Good even, Casca. Brought you Caesar home?　1
Why are you breathless? and why stare you so?
Casca. Are you not moved when all the sway of　3
　　earth
Shakes like a thing infirm? O Cicero,
I have seen tempests when the scolding winds
Have rived the knotty oaks, and I have seen　6
Th' ambitious ocean swell and rage and foam
To be exalted with the threat'ning clouds;
But never till to-night, never till now,
Did I go through a tempest dropping fire.　10
Either there is a civil strife in heaven,
Or else the world, too saucy with the gods,
Incenses them to send destruction.
Cicero. Why, saw you anything more wonderful?
Casca. A common slave (you know him well by sight)
Held up his left hand, which did flame and burn
Like twenty torches joined; and yet his hand,
Not sensible of fire, remained unscorched.　18
Besides (I ha' not since put up my sword),

---

299. "quick mettle": sharp.

302. "puts . . . form": pretends to be slow and simple.

310. "the world": i.e., the Roman world.

312. "wrought": worked on, changed.

313. "that . . . disposed": its natural inclination.

314. "with their likes": with those that think as they do.

316. "bear me hard": bears me a grudge.

318. "humour": persuade by flattery. Lines 317-8 have been variously interpreted. They may mean i) If I were Brutus and Brutus were Cassius, he would not persuade me, or ii) If I were Brutus and Caesar were Cassius, Caesar would not persuade me. The interpretation is of some importance. The first, which seems also the likeliest, puts Cassius (at least at this point in the play) in a particularly cynical and cold-blooded light.

319. "several hands": different handwritings.

321-2. "great opinion That": great respect in which.

323. "ambition": for the Elizabethans the word had the special meaning of unscrupulous pursuit of power. "glanced at": hinted at.

Stage Direction "Thunder and lightning": Thunder was provided in the Elizabethan theater by beating a piece of metal backstage. The lightning is provided in the language, e.g., Casca's "tempest dropping fire."

1. "Brought": escorted.

3. "sway": established order.

6. "rived": split in two.

10. "dropping fire": thunderbolts. In this and what follows Shakespeare may be adapting Plutarch's suggestion that before Caesar's assassination "divers men were seen going up and down in the fire."

18. "Not sensible": unable to feel.

JULIUS CAESAR

ACT I SCENE III

create, as the electricians cannot, many different kinds, or variations, of night and darkness. It may be the romantic night which surrounds the lovers in the last Act of THE MERCHANT OF VENICE, where

> The moon shines bright: in such a night as this
>
> When the sweet wind did gently kiss the trees . . .

Or it may be evil, as is the night in which Lady Macbeth contemplates the murder of Duncan

> Come thick night,
>
> And pall me in the dunnest smoke of hell,
>
> That my keen knife sees not the wound it makes . . .

Or it may be ominous and terrifying, as in this scene,

> this dreadful night
>
> That thunders, lightens, opens graves, and roars
>
> As doth the lion in the Capitol . . .

Night provides an important atmospheric, or symbolic setting in Shakespeare: it is often associated with malevolence or evil. Here, as in MACBETH, night provides an appropriate background for the lurking, plotting conspirators. It also suggests, as Brutus says in II,i, a time "when evil is most free." The storm is also important, and the stage directions remind us that it continues through this scene, through the next scene with Brutus, and to the scene after that, with Caesar, thus linking the three together. Storm in Shakespeare's plays carried a significance that is largely lost for us. The Elizabethans thought of individual man, his society (or "the state"), and the natural world as intimately and indivisibly connected. Therefore disorder and violence in the world of nature suggested, and on the stage could represent, disorder in the society and the individual. For the Elizabethans the king symbolized the state, and therefore when the king is murdered (i.e., when the social order is violently disrupted) in MACBETH, we have a storm ("the heavens, as troubled by man's act/Threaten his bloody stage") much like the storm here, with its "monstrous prodigies." In both cases violence, murder, and consequent social disorder, are at hand. In the same way the individual was often compared to nature, and to society: disorder in one might be used to express disorder in the other. Thus when Brutus agonizes over his part in the plot against Caesar he compares himself to a society in conflict:

> the state of man,
>
> Like to a little kingdom, suffers then
>
> The nature of an insurrection.
> (II,i,67)

Against the Capitol I met a lion,
Who glazed upon me, and went surly by   21
Without annoying me. And there were drawn   22
Upon a heap a hundred ghastly women,   23
Transformed with their fear, who swore they saw
Men, all in fire, walk up and down the streets.
And yesterday the bird of night did sit   26
Even at noonday upon the market place,
Hooting and shrieking. When these prodigies   28
Do so conjointly meet, let not men say
'These are their reasons—they are natural,'
For I believe they are portentous things
Unto the climate that they point upon.   32
   Cicero. It is indeed a strange-disposed time
But men may construe things after their fashion,   34
Clean from the purpose of the things themselves.   35
Comes Caesar to the Capitol to-morrow?
   Casca. He doth; for he did bid Antonius
Send word to you he would be there to-morrow.
   Cicero. Good night then, Casca. This disturb'd sky
Is not to walk in.
   Casca.   Farewell, Cicero.   [*Exit* CICERO.
              Enter CASSIUS.
   Cassius. Who's there?
   Casca.   A Roman.
   Cassius.   Casca, by your voice.
   Casca. Your ear is good. Cassius, what night is this!
   Cassius. A very pleasing night to honest men.
   Casca. Who ever knew the heavens menace so?
   Cassius. Those that have known the earth so full of faults.
For my part, I have walked about the streets,
Submitting me unto the perilous night,
And, thus unbraced, Casca, as you see,   48
Have bared my bosom to the thunder-stone;   49
And when the cross blue lightning seemed to open   50
The breast of heaven, I did present myself
Even in the aim and very flash of it.
   Casca. But wherefore did you so much tempt the heavens?
It is the part of men to fear and tremble   54
When the most mighty gods by tokens send
Such dreadful heralds to astonish us.   56
   Cassius. You are dull, Casca, and those sparks of life
That should be in a Roman you do want,
Or else you use not. You look pale, and gaze,
And put on fear, and cast yourself in wonder,   60
To see the strange impatience of the heavens;
But if you would consider the true cause—
Why all these fires, why all these gliding ghosts,
Why birds and beasts, from quality and kind;   64
Why old men, fools, and children calculate;   65
Why all these things change from their ordinance,   66
Their natures, and preformed faculties,   67
To monstrous quality—why you shall find   68
That heaven hath infused them with these spirits
To make them instruments of fear and warning
Unto some monstrous state.   71
Now could I, Casca, name to thee a man
Most like this dreadful night

---

21. "glazed": a combination of glared and gazed.

22-3. "drawn . . . heap": huddled together.

26. "bird of night": the owl, also taken from Plutarch.

28. "prodigies": unnatural events.

32. "climate": country or region.

34. "construe": explain (with the accent on the first syllable).

35. "clean . . . purpose": at variance with the real meaning.

48. "unbraced": with doublet untied.

49. "thunder-stone": thunderbolt, lightning.

50. "cross": forked.

54. "part": natural action.

56. "astonish": to stun (originally, with a stone), to terrify.

60. "cast . . . wonder": throw yourself into a state of wonder.

64. "from . . . kind": changed in their nature.

65. "calculate": make prophecies.

66. "ordinance": natural order.

67. "preformed": innate.

68. "monstrous": unnatural.

71. "Unto . . . state": of some terrible happening.

JULIUS CAESAR

ACT I SCENE III

(For more on this Elizabethan point of view, which is important to the understanding of Shakespeare, but too complex to deal with properly here, see E.M.W. Tillyard, THE ELIZABETHAN WORLD PICTURE, and T. Spencer, SHAKESPEARE AND THE NATURE OF MAN).

Since the actual violence of the storm cannot be reproduced on the Elizabethan stage Shakespeare, as usual, communicates it through the effect it has on a character. Casca, running onto the stage with a drawn sword, says that "all the sway of earth/Shakes like a thing infirm," and goes on to give a vivid evocation of the tempest that we cannot see but can, with him, imagine. Note that Casca here speaks in blank verse rather than the prose we had associated with him in I,ii. The reason for this is twofold. Firstly, the kind of terrifying and supernatural occurrences treated here need the special elevation and rhythmic incantation of poetry. Secondly, it is significant that it should be Casca, hitherto represented as tough and unimpressionable, who is so shaken by these nocturnal omens; it gives them added force for us.

The imagery throughout this passage (ll. 3-28) has an intense and nightmarish quality. The "tempest dropping fire" is no ordinary lightning storm, and is followed by the figure of a man holding up his hand "which did flame and burn /Like twenty torches joined." This image, and that of the lion which follows it, are both associated in our minds with destruction or violence, and these are in turn followed by a powerful suggestion of general terror and desolation in the "hundred ghastly women/ Transformed with their fear" whom Casca next sees. The passage ends with the owl, "the bird of night," a traditional omen of evil for the Elizabethan audience.

That thunders, lightens, opens graves, and roars
As doth the lion in the Capitol;
A man no mightier than thyself or me
In personal action, yet prodigious grown
And fearful, as these strange eruptions are.
    Casca. 'Tis Caesar that you mean. Is it not, Cassius?
    Cassius. Let it be who it is. For Romans now
Have thews and limbs like to their ancestors;
But woe the while! our fathers' minds are dead,   82
And we are governed with other mothers' spirits;
Our yoke and sufferance show us womanish.   84
    Casca. Indeed, they say the senators to-morrow
Mean to establish Caesar as a king,
And he shall wear his crown by sea and land
In every place save here in Italy.   88
    Cassius. I know where I will wear this dagger then;   89
Cassius from bondage will deliver Cassius.
Therein, ye gods, you make the weak most strong;   91
Therein, ye gods, you tyrants do defeat.
Nor stony tower, nor walls of beaten brass,
Nor airless dungeon, nor strong links of iron,
Can be retentive to the strength of spirit;   95
But life, being weary of these worldly bars,
Never lacks power to dismiss itself.
If I know this, know all the world besides,   98
That part of tyranny that I do bear
I can shake off at pleasure.   [*Thunder still.*
    Casca.   So can I.
So every bondman in his own hand bears
The power to cancel his captivity.
    Cassius. And why should Caesar be a tyrant then?
Poor man! I know he would not be a wolf
But that he sees the Romans are but sheep;
He were no lion, were not Romans hinds.   106
Those that with haste will make a mighty fire
Behind it with weak straws. What trash is Rome,
What rubbish and what offal, when it serves   109
For the base matter to illuminate   110
So vile a thing as Caesar! But, O grief,
Where hast thou led me? I, perhaps, speak this
Before a willing bondman. Then I know
My answer must be made. But I am armed,   114
And dangers are to me indifferent.   115
    Casca. You speak to Casca, and to such a man
That is no fleering telltale. Hold, my hand.   117
Be factious for redress of all these griefs,   118
And I will set this foot of mine as far
As who goes farthest.   [*They shake hands.*
    Cassius.   There's a bargain made.
Now know you, Casca, I have moved already
Some certain of the noblest-minded Romans
To undergo with me an enterprise
Of honourable dangerous consequence;
And I do know, by this, they stay for me   125
In Pompey's Porch; for now, this fearful night,   126
There is no stir or walking in the streets,
And the complexion of the element   128
Is fev'rous, like the work we have in hand,   129
Most bloody, fiery, and most terrible.

82. "woe the while": alas for this age.

84. "yoke and sufferance": i.e., meek endurance of tyranny.

88. i.e., anywhere in the Roman Empire except Italy itself (which would presumably still be too powerfully republican to permit this).

89. i.e., he will sheathe it in his own body.

91. "therein": i.e., in suicide.

95. "Can . . . to": can confine.

98. "know . . . world": let all the world know.

106. "hinds": deer, with an Elizabethan pun on servants.

109. "offal": waste.

110. "illuminate": give light to, in the sense of making famous.

114. "My . . . made": i.e., I shall have to defend what I have said.

115. "indifferent": a matter of indifference.

117. "fleering": the Elizabethan meaning combined our fawning and sneering.

118. "factious": active.

125. "by this": i.e., because of the storm.

126. "Pompey's Porch": the colonnade of the theater built by Pompey.

128. "complexion . . . element": appearance of the sky.

129. "fev'rous": feverish.

JULIUS CAESAR

ACT I SCENE III

Professor Wilson Knight has shown the way in which the ideas and images of music and storm recur in Shakespeare's plays in such a way that the first is associated with goodness and harmony, the second with evil and strife. We were told in scene two that Cassius "hears no music" (see glossary I,ii,204, and we are not surprised now when he welcomes the storm (l. 43). It reflects his own mood of overpowering, destructive anger. He sees it, as he sees everything at this point in the play, in relation to Caesar, and he takes advantage of Casca's fear to enlist him among the conspirators. Notice that once this has been done, both behave with an obviously tense, conspiratorial quality. They are afraid to be seen ("Stand close") when Cinna enters, and once they recognize him and all draw together the dialogue is conducted with nervous urgency (ll. 134 ff.). Cinna wants to be certain who Casca is, Cassius has to repeat his question to Cinna, and finally Cassius gives his orders concerning the letters to Brutus in brief, hurried phrases. The conspirators have completed their plans to make Brutus a central figure in their plot, but as they congratulate themselves on this, Shakespeare adds a typical touch of dramatic irony to indicate how misplaced their optimism is (see glossary, l. 159).

ACT II SCENE I

The stormy night continues, and Brutus' first lines refer to the surrounding darkness. Darkness throughout this scene is given a subtle but important symbolic significance. It represents, or suggests imaginatively, the darkness and the confusion in Brutus' mind. Later on the conspirators arrive in darkness, and one feels that night (and its association with secrecy and evil) gives a sinister quality to everything they say and do. Compare the same effect when Macbeth plots the murder of Duncan:

Now o'er one half the world
Nature seems dead, and wicked
  dreams abuse
The curtained sleep.

Enter CINNA.

Casca. Stand close awhile, for here comes one in 131
  haste.
Cassius. 'Tis Cinna. I do know him by his gait.
He is a friend. Cinna, where haste you so?
Cinna. To find out you. Who's that? Metellus
  Cimber?
Cinna. No, it is Casca, one incorporate 135
To our attempts. Am I not stayed for, Cinna? 136
Cinna. I am glad on't. What a fearful night is this! 137
There's two or three of us have seen strange sights.
Cassius. Am I not stayed for? Tell me.
Cinna.   Yes, you are.
O Cassius, if you could
But win the noble Brutus to our party—
Cassius. Be you content. Good Cinna, take this paper
And look you lay it in the praetor's chair, 143
Where Brutus may but find it. And throw this
In at his window. Set this up with wax
Upon old Brutus' statue. All this done, 146
Repair to Pompey's Porch, where you shall find us.
Is Decius Brutus and Trebonius there? 148
Cinna. All but Metellus Cimber, and he's gone
To seek you at your house. Well, I will hie 150
And so bestow the papers as you bade me.
Cassius. That done, repair to Pompey's Theatre.
                                      [*Exit* CINNA.
Come, Casca, you and I will yet ere day
See Brutus at his house. Three parts of him
Is ours already, and the man entire
Upon the next encounter yields him ours.
Casca. O, he sits high in all the people's hearts;
And that which would appear offence in us,
His countenance, like richest alchemy, 159
Will change to virtue and to worthiness.
Cassius. Him and his worth and our great need of
  him
You have right well conceited. Let us go, 162
For it is after midnight; and ere day
We will awake him and be sure of him. [*Exeunt.*

ACT TWO, scene one.

(BRUTUS' ORCHARD.)

Enter BRUTUS.

Brutus. What, Lucius, ho!
I cannot by the progress of the stars
Give guess how near to day. Lucius I say!
I would it were my fault to sleep so soundly.
When, Lucius, when? Awake, I say! What, Lucius! 5
Enter LUCIUS.
Lucius. Called you, my lord?
Brutus. Get me a taper in my study, Lucius. 7
When it is lighted, come and call me here.
Lucius. I will, my lord. [*Exit.*
Brutus. It must be by his death; and for my part,
I know no personal cause to spurn at him, 11

---

131. "Stand close": stand back, conceal yourself.

135-6. "incorporate To": part of.

137. "glad on't": Cinna's answer is to the news that Casca is one of the conspirators. Cassius repeats his question.

143. "praetor": magistrate; an office at this time held by Brutus.

146. "old Brutus' statue": see I,ii,159.

148. "Decius Brutus": a relative of Brutus.

150. "hie": hurry.

159. "His countenance": i) his face, ii) his approval.
"alchemy": the alchemists tried to change base metals into gold. Whenever Shakespeare uses the word it is associated with the failure, or falsity of this pseudo-science. Thus its effect in Casca's speech is unconsciously ironic. Although Casca cannot know it yet, the addition of Brutus does not change the conspirator's plot "to virtue and to worthiness."

162. "well conceited": both correctly conceived and aptly expressed.

5. "When . . . when . . . What": exclamations of impatience.

7. "taper": candle.

11. "spurn": kick at.

JULIUS CAESAR

ACT II SCENE I

Brutus calls to Lucius, his servant boy, for light. Here too some critics have seen symbolic significance. Brutus, in a darkness both actual and mental, asks the boy for illumination. Lucius' name is derived from the Latin word for light (LUCERE: to light), and in a sense he represents the illumination, or understanding, that Brutus needs. Yet Brutus never reaches the "light" provided by Lucius in the study; instead he is interrupted by the conspirators, coming "by night /When evils are most free." Throughout the play Lucius, although a minor character, is important in that he shows us the serenity and peace of mind that Brutus has lost. Sleep in Shakesphere is often associated with peace, and Lucius can sleep when Brutus cannot (both here, and at IV,iii,267). Brutus, awake and harassed by anxiety, half-recognizes the contrast between Lucius' innocent sleep and his own guilty wakefulness when he compares "the honey-heavy dew of slumber" with the "fantasies" and "busy cares" that plague him (ll.230-2). Brutus' dealings with the boy (and with Portia) reflect his gentleness and humanity. Some directors of the play have given Lucius the part of Strato, so that, at the end of the play, it is Lucius who holds the sword on which Brutus kills himself, i.e., he finally provides that "sleep" of peace which is the only thing that Brutus, broken and defeated, really desires.

Brutus' soliloquy (beginning at l. 10) is an important one. It is an example of Shakespeare's brilliance in revealing ambiguous or confused states of mind, where the confusion or ambiguity is not clearly realized by the speaker himself. The heroes of Shakespeare's tragedies are often in the position of making decisions which will ultimately destroy them, and the real nature of which they do not themselves understand. By the language they use, Shakespeare manages to suggest both their surface certainty, and their unconscious doubt or confusion. In this speech Brutus seems certain of what he has to do. He begins, in fact, with a final decision: "It must be by his death." But when he proceeds to his reasons, or justifications, Shakespeare makes them doubtful, although plausible. Brutus, the man of honor, says he has no "personal cause" for destroying Caesar (and we compare him with Cassius, whose personal animosity was made clear in I,ii). Brutus goes on to say that Caesar must die because he will abuse his power. Yet he adds at once that he has no evidence that Caesar ever behaved unreasonably. The two remarks about "bright day" bringing forth "the adder," and "young

But for the general. He would be crowned. 12
How that might change his nature, there the question.
It is the bright day that brings forth the adder, 14
And that craves wary walking. Crown him that 15
And then I grant we put a sting in him
That at his will he may do danger with.
Th' abuse of greatness is, when it disjoins
Remorse from power. And to speak truth of Caesar 19
I have not known when his affections swayed 20
More than his reason. But 'tis common proof 21
That lowliness is young ambition's ladder, 22
Whereto the climber upward turns his face;
But when he once attains the upmost round,
He then unto the ladder turns his back,
Looks in the clouds, scorning the base degrees 26
By which he did ascend. So Caesar may.
Then lest he may, prevent. And since the quarrel
Will bear no colour for the thing he is, 29
Fashion it thus: that what he is, augmented, 30
Would run to these and these extremities; 31
And therefore think him as a serpent's egg,
Which, hatched, would as his kind grow mischievous 33
And kill him in the shell.

Enter LUCIUS.

Lucius. The taper burneth in your closet, sir. 35
Searching the window for a flint, I found
This paper, thus sealed up; and I am sure
It did not lie there when I went to bed.
　　　　　　　　　　　　[*Gives him a letter.*
Brutus. Get you to bed again; it is not day.
Is not to-morrow, boy, the ides of March?
Lucius. I know not, sir.
Brutus. Look in the calendar and bring me word.
Lucius. I will, sir.
Brutus. These exhalations, whizzing in the air, 44
Gives so much light that I may read by them.
　　　　　　　　　[*Opens the letter and reads.*
'Brutus, thou sleep'st. Awake and see thyself!
Shall Rome, &c. Speak, strike, redress!' 47
Brutus, thou sleep'st. Awake!
Such instigations have been often dropped
Where I have took them up.
'Shall Rome, &c.' Thus must I piece it out:
Shall Rome stand under one man's awe? What, Rome?
My ancestors did from the streets of Rome
The Tarquin drive when he was called a king.
'Speak, strike, redress!' Am I entreated
To speak and strike? O Rome, I make thee promise,
If the redress will follow, thou receivest
Thy full petition at the hand of Brutus. 58

Enter LUCIUS.

Lucius. Sir, March is wasted fifteen days.
　　　　　　　　　　　[*Knock within.* s.d.
Brutus. 'Tis good. Go to the gate; somebody knocks.
　　　　　　　　　　　　[*Exit Lucius.*
Since Cassius first did whet me against Caesar,
I have not slept.
Between the acting of a dreadful thing
And the first motion, all the interim is
Like a phantasma or a hideous dream. 65
The genius and the mortal instruments 66

12. "the general": general reasons in the interest of the public good.

14-15. "It . . . walking": i.e., the sunshine brings out the adder and makes careful walking necessary.

15. "Crown him that": Brutus hesitates at the distasteful word king.

19. "Remorse": the word meant mercy or humanity in a general sense to the Elizabethans.

20. "affections swayed": passions ruled.

21. "common proof": common experience.

22. "lowliness": false humility.

26. "base degrees": both i) rungs of the ladder, and ii) lower ranks.

29. "colour": excuse.
"he": it.

30. "Fashion": shape, change the form of.

31. "extremities": extremes of power.

33. "his kind": his nature.

35. "closet": study.

44. "exhalations": meteors. Brutus recalls to the audience that the storm continues; it underlines the tension throughout the scene. See commentary at I,iii.

47. "&c.": and so on. The ampersand sign allows the actor to ad lib the action of reading to himself.

58. "thy full petition": all you ask.

Stage Direction "within": i.e., offstage.

65. phantasma": horrible illusion.

66. "genius . . . instruments": spirit and faculties.

ACT II SCENE I

ambition's ladder" both have the quality of conventional phrases: they are plausible excuses, not logical arguments. Then Brutus significantly admits that the "quarrel" really HAS no "colour"—or excuse—as it stands. He is compelled to "fashion it," or put it in some other, more acceptable way. And he ends by unconsciously admitting that in order to be able to act he must, in a sense, distort his view of Caesar: "therefore think of him as the serpent's egg." As Brutus argues with (and convinces) himself, we realize, through the language Shakespeare gives him, the basic uncertainty of his position.

Lines 55-8 are understood ironically by the audience, though not by Brutus. "Redress" means revenge, and "thy full petition" means that Rome will get from Brutus all it asks for. This is true in a sense other than Brutus intends; what Rome will ultimately ask for is Brutus' life.

As Lucius leaves to bring in Cassius and the other conspirators Brutus' speech (ll. 76-85) indicates the way in which he, the model of moral rectitude, has compromised himself. Throughout the play he insists (and we believe him) on his integrity and honesty, and, as he says here, conspiracy is ashamed to show its "monstrous visage" and must "hide in smiles and affability." We remember this, as Brutus advances to greet the conspirators and make himself one of them. He is himself now among the "secret Romans," and we wonder how this new role will square with his morality.

At line 100 Brutus and Cassius withdraw, presumably while Cassius makes sure Brutus' support. Meanwhile Decius, Casca and Cinna talk, apparently quite irrelevantly, about which direction the sun will rise. As with many apparent irrelevancies in Shakespeare, this has dramatic value. Men under extreme stress frequently ease themselves with this kind of aimless talk, and the references to the rising of the sun ("Doth not the day break here?"), like the reference to the ides of March, earlier, sharpens the dramatic anticipation of the audience: the day of the assassination is beginning.

Are then in council, and the state of man,
Like to a little kingdom, suffers then
The nature of an insurrection.

       Enter LUCIUS.

Lucius. Sir, 'tis your brother Cassius at the door, 70
Who doth desire to see you.
Brutus.   Is he alone?
Lucius. No, sir. There are moe with him. 72
Brutus.   Do you know them?
Lucius. No, sir. Their hats are plucked about
   their ears
And half their faces buried in their cloaks,
That by no means I may discover them
By any mark of favour. 76
Brutus.   Let 'em enter.   [*Exit* LUCIUS.
They are the faction. O conspiracy,
Sham'st thou to show thy dangerous brow by night,
When evils are most free? O, then by day
Where wilt thou find a cavern dark enough
To mask thy monstrous visage? Seek none, conspiracy.
Hide it in smiles and affability:
For if thou put thy native semblance on, 83
Not Erebus itself were dim enough 84
To hide thee from prevention. 85

   Enter the conspirators, CASSIUS, CASCA, DECIUS, CINNA,
      METELLUS CIMBER, *and* TREBONIUS.

Cassius. I think we are too bold upon your rest.
Good morrow, Brutus. Do we trouble you?
Brutus. I have been up this hour, awake all night.
Know I these men that come along with you?
Cassius. Yes, every man of them; and no man here
But honours you; and every one doth wish
You had but that opinion of yourself
Which every noble Roman bears of you.
This is Trebonius.
Brutus.   He is welcome hither.
Cassius. This, Decius Brutus.
Brutus.   He is welcome too.
Cassius. This, Casca; this, Cinna; and this Metellus
   Cimber.
Brutus. They are all welcome.
What watchful cares do interpose themselves 98
Betwixt your eyes and night?
Cassius. Shall I entreat a word?   [*They whisper.*
Decius. Here lies the east. Doth not the day break
   here?
Casca. No.
Cinna. O, pardon sir, it doth; and yon grey lines
That fret the clouds are messengers of day.
Casca. You shall confess that you are both deceived.
Here, as I point my sword, the sun arises,
Which is a great way growing on the south, 107
Weighing the youthful season of the year.
Some two months hence, up higher toward the north
He first presents his fire; and the high east
Stands as the Capitol, directly here.
Brutus. Give me your hands all over, one by one.
Cassius. And let us swear our resolution.
Brutus. No, not an oath. If not the face of men, 114
The sufferance of our souls, the time's abuse—

70. "brother": brother-in-law; Cassius had married Brutus' sister.

72. "moe": more.

76. "favour": feature.

83. "native semblance": natural appearance. Some editors read "path" (walk) for "put" in this line.

84. "Erebus": in classical mythology a region of darkness between Earth and Hades.

85. "prevention": being prevented or forestalled.

98. "watchful cares": cares that keep one awake.

107. "growing on": toward.

114-6. "if the misery in men's faces, the suffering in their souls, the evils of the time are not strong enough motives." (J. H. Walter)

JULIUS CAESAR

ACT II SCENE I

The conspirators now discuss their next moves (ll. 141-190), and here we watch Brutus make two judgments which i) tell us something about the man, and ii) by implication, suggest that the plot against Caesar is on unsure ground because of Brutus' judgment. We have already seen, in Cassius' and Brutus' analysis of Casca (I,ii), some of the differences between the two men: Cassius the practical intelligence "looking quite through the deeds of men," Brutus high-minded and utterly sincere, yet without the shrewdness to judge men's behavior, or the tactical requirements of political action. Cassius suggests that Cicero ought to be included, and Metellus seconds this, because the "good opinion" Rome has of Cicero "will commend our deeds." We have seen Cicero earlier, during the storm, where his calmness was in noticeable contrast to Casca's fear and excitement. Furthermore the name of Cicero stands, for the Elizabethans and for us, for intelligent Roman statesmanship. We feel that Metellus is right, but Brutus at once rejects his suggestion with the brisk "name him not!", followed by a reason that is doubtful at best. Next Cassius brings up the question of Mark Antony, observing with sour wit that since Antony and Caesar are so close, it seems a shame to let one outlive the other. Faced with the decision, Brutus makes what will prove to be a vital mistake. Since Antony is given "To sports, to wildness, and much company" he can be dismissed as a threat. Brutus is not only upright, he is also somewhat righteous, and like the righteous, often over simplifies characters unlike his own. In shrugging Antony off as an ineffectual plea-

If these be motives weak, break off betimes,   116
And every man hence to his idle bed.
So let high-sighted tyranny rage on   118
Till each man drop by lottery. But if these   119
(As I am sure they do) bear fire enough
To kindle cowards and to steel with valour
The melting spirits of women, then, countrymen,
What need we any spur but our own cause
To prick us to redress? what other bond   124
Than secret Romans that have spoke the word
And will not palter? and what other oath   126
Than honesty to honesty engaged
That this shall be, or we will fall for it?
Swear priests and cowards and men cautelous,   129
Old feeble carrions and such suffering souls   130
That welcome wrongs; unto bad causes swear
Such creatures as men doubt; but do not stain
The even virtue of our enterprise,
Nor th' insuppressive mettle of our spirits,   134
To think that or our cause or our performance
Did need an oath; when every drop of blood
That every Roman bears, and nobly bears,
Is guilty of a several bastardy   138
If he do break the smallest particle
Of any promise that hath passed from him.
  Cassius. But what of Cicero? Shall we sound him?
I think he will stand very strong with us.
  Casca. Let us not leave him out.
  Cinna.   No, by no means.
  Metellus. O, let us have him! for his silver hairs
Will purchase us a good opinion   145
And buy men's voices to commend our deeds.
It shall be said his judgment ruled our hands.
Our youths and wildness shall no whit appear,
But all be buried in his gravity.   149
  Brutus. O, name him not! Let us not break with 150
    him;
For he will never follow anything
That other men begin.
  Cassius.   Then leave him out.
  Casca. Indeed he is not fit.
  Decius. Shall no man else be touched but only
    Caesar?
  Cassius. Decius, well urged. I think it is not meet
Mark Antony, so well beloved of Caesar,
Should outlive Caesar. We shall find of him
A shrewd contriver; and you know, his means,   158
If he improve them, may well stretch so far
As to annoy us all; which, to prevent,
Let Antony and Caesar fall together.
  Brutus. Our course will seem too bloody, Caius
    Cassius,
To cut the head off and then hack the limbs,
Like wrath in death and envy afterwards;   164
For Antony is but a limb of Caesar.
Let's be sacrificers, but not butchers, Caius.
We all stand up against the spirit of Caesar,   167
And in the spirit of men there is no blood.
O that we then could come by Caesar's spirit
And not dismember Caesar! But, alas,
Caesar must bleed for it! And, gentle friends,

116. "betimes": at once.

118. "high-sighted"' ambitious.

119. "by lottery": by chance ("as the tyrant's gaze chances to light on him" —Arden edition).
"if these": i.e., these motives.

124. "prick": spur.

126. "palter": quibble or deceive.

129. "cautelous": crafty.

130. "carrions": living carcasses.

134. "insuppressive": unsuppressable, indomitable.

138. "several bastardy": i.e., a separate act, showing it not to be true Roman blood.

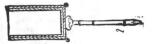

145. "opinion": reputation.

149. "gravity": authority.

150. "break with": break our news to, discuss.

158. "means': powers.

164. "envy": malice.

167. "spirit": i.e., that which Caesar stands for. The irony of the line lies in the fact that although Brutus means here that they will destroy the Caesar principle, the word also means ghost, and Caesar's ghost does return to haunt Brutus (IV,iii).

ACT II SCENE I

sure-seeker he makes a judgment that will return, quite literally, to haunt him (at IV,iii, 275). Cassius, on the other hand, rightly estimates the danger in Antony's "ingrafted love" for Caesar.

One other point occurs in this debate which further enlarges our understanding of Brutus. We know that he believes his part in the conspiracy to be morally justifiable; but we have also seen, in his soliloquy, something like uncertainty, or guilt, which he has tried to dispel. He must at all costs make the assassination an act of public morality. In the speech at lines 162-183 he introduces the idea of religious sacrifice. The conspirators will be "sacrificers, but not butchers" and "carve" Caesar in a way which is "fit for the gods,/Not hew him as a carcass fit for hounds." Brutus cannot stomach the deed if it is not performed as an almost religious duty. Again he seems to be trying to avoid, or not face directly, the violence and bloody nature of the deed. He does not want it to seem like a hunt, in which the carcass is fed to the hounds. We shall see later that this is exactly the metaphor that Antony uses in describing the dead Caesar, the "brave hart" surrounded by the "hunters" and "bloody butchers."

Let's kill him boldly, but not wrathfully;
Let's carve him as a dish fit for the gods,
Not hew him as a carcass fit for hounds.
And let our hearts, as subtle masters do,   175
Stir up their servants to an act of rage
And after seem to chide 'em. This shall make   177
Our purpose necessary, and not envious;   178
Which so appearing to the common eyes,
We shall be called purgers, not murderers.
And for Mark Antony, think not of him;
For he can do no more than Caesar's arm
When Caesar's head is off.
Cassius.   Yet I fear him;
For in the ingrafted love he bears to Caesar—   184
Brutus. Alas, good Cassius, do not think of him!
If he love Caesar, all that he can do
Is to himself—take thought, and die for Caesar.
And that were much he should; for he is given   188
To sports, to wildness, and much company.
Trebonius. There is no fear in him. Let him not die;   190
For he will live, and laugh at this hereafter.
                        [*Clock strikes.*
Brutus. Peace! Count the clock.
Cassius.   The clock hath stricken three.
Trebonius. 'Tis time to part.
Cassius.   But it is doubtful yet
Whether Caesar will come forth to-day or no;
For he is superstitious grown of late,
Quite from the main opinion he held once   196
Of fantasy, of dreams, and ceremonies.   197
It may be these apparent prodigies,   198
The unaccustomed terror of this night,
And the persuasion of his augurers   200
May hold him from the Capitol to-day.
Decius. Never fear that. If he be so resolved,
I can o'ersway him; for he loves to hear
That unicorns may be betrayed with trees   204
And bears with glasses, elephants with holes,   205
Lions with toils, and men with flatterers;   206
But when I tell him he hates flatterers,
He says he does, being then most flattered.
Let me work;
For I can give his humour the true bent   210
And I will bring him to the Capitol.
Cassius. Nay, we will all of us be there to fetch him.   212
Brutus. By the eighth hour. Is that the uttermost?   213
Cinna. Be that the uttermost, and fail not then.
Metellus. Caius Ligarius doth bear Caesar hard,   215
Who rated him for speaking well of Pompey.   216
I wonder none of you have thought of him.
Brutus. Now, good Metellius, go along by him.   218
He loves me well, and I have given him reasons
Send him but hither, and I'll fashion him.   220
Cassius. The morning comes upon 's. We'll leave
    you, Brutus.
And, friends, disperse yourselves; but all remember
What we have said and show yourselves true Romans.
Brutus. Good gentlemen, look fresh and merrily.
Let not our looks put on our purposes,   225
But bear it as our Roman actors do,
With untired spirits and formal constancy.   227

175-7. "And . . . 'em": i.e., let our hearts excite our hands to an act of violence, and afterwards rebuke them.

178. "envious": malicious.

184. "ingrafted": deep-rooted.

188. "And . . . should": i.e., that is too much to expect of him.

190. "no fear": nothing to fear.

196. "from the main": as opposed to the strong.

197. "ceremonies": portents, omens.

198. "apparent prodigies": wonders that have appeared.

200. "augurers": priests who interpreted omens.

204. "betrayed with trees": i.e., tricked into running their horns into trees, and thus easily captured.

205. "glasses": mirrors, in which they think they see other bears.
"holes": pits as traps.

206. "toils": snares.
"flatterers": i.e., flatterers are to men as the various snares are to animals.

210. "humour . . . bent": i.e., I can guide his mood.

212. "fetch": escort.

213. "uttermost": latest.

215. "bear Caesar hard": bear a grudge against Caesar.

216. "rated": upbraided.

218. "by him": to his house.

220. "fashion": shape· (to our purpose).

225. "put on": reveal.

227. "formal constancy": steadfast self-possession.

JULIUS CAESAR

ACT II SCENE I

The conspirators leave, and Brutus is left alone with Lucius. Brutus turns to command the boy something, but finding him asleep he relents, and compares the boy's peace to his own turmoil, as Portia enters. Between them Portia and Lucius suggest to us all that is, or might have been, normal and happy in Brutus' life. They stand as a contrast to the world of the conspiracy, the struggles of conscience, and the violence of assassination and battle. Lucius we have already discussed, but Portia requires some comment.

The play is predominantly about men, and their struggle for power, and therefore a large part of it is concerned with debate, planning and battle. Brutus appears most of the time as a public figure, surrounded by men and concerned in affairs of state. But in order to give depth and humanity to his character Shakespeare introduces Portia, so that we may see Brutus in a very different context: a man who has a home, and a wife whom he loves, and who loves him.

Women's parts were, of course, taken by boys on the Elizabethan stage, and this presented a problem to the dramatist. He was obliged to keep his female characters relatively simple, since a boy-actor could not be expected to do justice to the complex moods and emotions of a Prince Hamlet or a King Lear. It is true that Shakespeare has, on at least two occasions, given us women of great power; but even Lady Macbeth and Cleopatra, impressive as they are, are far simpler, as characters, than most of the male creations. Making, as usual, a virtue out of necessity, Shakespeare converts the youth and limitations of his boy-actors into heroines who are simple, straightforward, and innocent: Cordelia, Desdemona, Miranda, and here, Portia.

In this scene Portia also reminds us, by her love and solicitude for her troubled husband, that Brutus has been happy and contented in a period before our play began. This gives added pathos to the desperate and destructive course he now seems to have taken. When the death of Portia herself is announced, later in the play, we realize more fully the dimensions of the destruction he has brought about. Brutus' tragedy is both a public one (in effect, he destroys the thing he is trying to preserve—for republican freedom falls to the domination of the triumvirate) and a private one—the death of Portia, and his happiness. It is the private aspect of the tragedy that is prepared for in this scene.

And so good morrow to you every one.

[*Exeunt all except* BRUTUS.

Boy! Lucius! Fast asleep? It is no matter.
Enjoy the honey-heavy due of slumber.
Thou has no figures nor no fantasies   231
Which busy care draws in the brains of men;
Therefore thou sleep'st so sound.

Enter PORTIA.

Portia.   Brutus, my lord.
Brutus. Portia! What mean you? Wherefore rise
    you now?
It is not for your health thus to commit   235
Your weak condition to the raw cold morning.   236
Portia. Nor for yours neither. Y' have ungently, 237
    Brutus,
Stole from my bed. And yesternight at supper
You suddenly arose and walked about,
Musing and sighing with your arms across: 240
And when I asked you what the matter was,
You stared upon me with ungentle looks.
I urged you further; then you scratched your head
And too impatiently stamped with your foot.
Yet I insisted; yet you answered not,
But with an angry wafter of your hand   246
Gave sign for me to leave you. So I did,
Fearing to strengthen that impatience
Which seemed too much enkindled, and withal
Hoping it was but an effect of humor,   250
Which sometime hath his hour with every man.
It will not let you eat nor talk nor sleep,
And could it work so much upon your shape   253
As it hath much prevailed on your condition,   254
I should not know you Brutus. Dear my lord,
Make me acquainted with your cause of grief.
Brutus. I am not well in health, and that is all.
Portia. Brutus is wise and, were he not in health,
He would embrace the means to come by it.
Brutus. Why so I do. Good Portia, go to bed.
Portia. Is Brutus sick, and is it physical   261
To walk unbraced and suck up the humours   262
Of the dank morning? What, is Brutus sick,
And will he steal out of his wholesome bed
To dare the vile contagion of the night,   265
And tempt the rheumy and unpurged air,   266
To add unto his sickness? No, my Brutus.
You have some sick offence within your mind,   268
Which by the right and virtue of my place
I ought to know of; and upon my knees
I charm you, by my once commended beauty,   271
By all your vows of love; and that great vow
Which did incorporate and make us one,   273
That you unfold to me, your self, your half,   274
Why you are heavy—and what men to-night
Have had resort to you; for here have been
Some six or seven, who did hide their faces
Even from darkness.
Brutus.   Kneel not, gentle Portia.
Portia. I should not need if you were gentle Brutus.
Within the bond of marriage, tell me, Brutus, 280
It is excepted I should know no secrets
That appertain to you? Am I your self

231. "figures": i.e., the mind, fantasies.

235. "commit": expose.

236. "condition": constitution.

237. "ungently": discourteously.

240. "across": folded across your chest, held by the Elizabethans to be a sign of melancholy.

246. "wafter": wave.

250. "humor": here, ill-humor.

253. "shape": physical appearance.

254. "condition": state of mind.

261. "physical": healthy.

262. "unbraced": with the doublet open. "humours": mists.

265. Night air was thought to be unhealthy. There is also a reference here, although Portia does not know it, to the night, or darkness, of conspiracy.

266. "rheumy": moist. "unpurged": not yet purified by the sun.

268. "sick offence": harmful illness.

271. "charm": means both i) persuade and ii) charm with her beauty.

273. "incorporate": join together.

274. "half": i.e., other half.

280-3. "bond," "excepted," "sort or limitation": these are all Elizabethan legal terms. The meaning is, is it part of the marriage contract that I should not know your secrets? Am I only a limited part of you?

JULIUS CAESAR

ACT II SCENE I

Portia reminds Brutus that she is Cato's daughter, and Cato the Elder has always served as a symbol of Roman fortitude and courage. At line 300 Shakespeare incorporates into Portia's speech a detail taken from Plutarch, and meant to exemplify the sort of stern self-discipline associated with Cato. This is the "voluntary wound" which, according to Plutarch, Portia gave herself to convince Brutus of her loyalty. "She took a razor, and causing her maids and women to go out of her chamber, she gave herself a great gash in her thigh, that she was straight covered with blood . . . and spake in this sort to Brutus: 'I being, Brutus, the daughter of Cato, was married to thee not to be thy bed-fellow and companion at board only, but to be partaker with thee of good and evil fortune . . . I have found that no pain and grief can overcome me.' With these words she showed him her wound, and told him what she had done to prove herself. Brutus besought the gods that he might be found a husband worthy of so noble a wife as Portia." (Plutarch: LIFE OF BRUTUS) Shakespeare takes the character of Portia straight from Plutarch's account; but notice the way he minimizes the details of the "voluntary wound," and enlarges on the humanity and tenderness of Brutus' wife.

But, as it were, in sort or limitation?   283
To keep with you at meals, comfort your bed,
And talk to you sometimes? Dwell I but in the
   suburbs   285
Of your good pleasure? If it be no more,
Portia is Brutus' harlot, not his wife.
  Brutus. You are my true and honourable wife,
As dear to me as are the ruddy drops
That visit my sad heart.
  Portia. If this were true, then should I know this
   secret.
I grant I am a woman; but withal
A woman that Lord Brutus took to wife.
I grant I am a woman; but withal
A woman well-reputed, Cato's daughter.   295
Think you I am no stronger than my sex,
Being so fathered and so husbanded?
Tell me your counsels; I will not disclose 'em.   298
I have made strong proof of my constancy,   299
Giving myself a voluntary wound
Here, in the thigh. Can I bear that with patience,
And not my husband's secrets?
  Brutus.   O ye gods,
Render me worthy of this noble wife!
                  [*Knocking within.*
Hark! hark! One knocks. Portia, go in awhile,
And by and by thy bosom shall partake
The secrets of my heart.
All my engagements I will construe thee,   307
And all the charactery of my sad brows.   308
Leave me with haste.   [*Exit* PORTIA.
    Lucius, who's that knocks?

Enter LUCIUS *and* CAIUS LIGARIUS.

  Lucius. Here is a sick man that would speak with
   you.
  Brutus. Caius Ligarius, that Metellus spake of.
Boy stand aside. Caius Ligarius, how?   312
  Caius. Vouchsafe good morrow from a feeble tongue.
  Brutus. O, what a time have you chose out, brave
   Caius,
To wear a kerchief! Would you were not sick!   315
  Caius. I am not sick if Brutus have in hand
Any exploit worthy the name of honour.
  Brutus. Such an exploit have I in hand, Ligarius,
Had you a healthful ear to hear of it.
  Cassius. By all the gods that Romans bow before,
I here discard my sickness. [*Throws off his ker-*
  chief] Soul of Rome,
Brave son derived from honourable loins,   322
Thou like an exorcist hast conjured up   323
My mortified spirit. Now bid me run,   324
And I will strive with things impossible;
Yea, get the better of them. What's to do?
  Brutus. A piece of work that will make sick men
   whole.   327
  Caius. But are not some whole that we must make
   sick?
  Brutus. That must we also. What it is, my Caius,
I shall unfold to thee as we are going,

285. "suburbs": London suburbs, notorious for prostitution. This idea introduces "harlot" in l. 287.

295. "Cato": Cato the Elder was famous for his stern morality; he fought with Pompey against Caesar and, defeated, killed himself.

298. "counsels": secret plans.

299. "proof of constancy": test of endurance.

307. "engagements": commitments.

308. "charactery": what is written upon, i.e., the meaning.

312. "how?": exclamation of surprise.

315. "wear a kerchief": i.e., wear some sort of bandage, be ill.

322. "derived . . . loins": of honorable descent.

323. "exorcist": magician.

324. "mortified": as though dead.

327. "whole": well. Brutus extends Ligarius' idea of recovery from sickness to the conspiracy.

ACT II SCENE I

What do you think is the significance of the Ligarius episode which ends the scene? Is Ligarius' recovery from his illness some sort of miraculous testimony to the healing qualities of Brutus? Or are we meant to understand, on the other hand, that just because of his nobility Brutus' enthusiasm may be a little TOO catching? Is there not more emotion than reason in Ligarius' statement that, so long as it is Brutus who leads, he will follow "To do I know not what"?

ACT II SCENE II

The stage direction calling for thunder and lightning joins Scenes i and ii. The storm beneath which Brutus and Caius Ligarius leave the stage continues as Caesar enters, and the symbolic association of the storm with violence in the world of men is present again at the beginning of this scene. The two scenes are linked in another way. We have just seen Brutus and Portia; now we have Caesar and his wife, Calpurnia. In both cases the women are apprehensive: Portia senses intuitively that something is wrong, and Calpurnia has had a frightening dream. In both cases the men disregard their wives, and proceed along their chosen courses of action, toward their fatal meeting.

Calpurnia's recital of the "horrid sights seen by the watch" intensifies our anticipation of the events to come, and is another example of Shakespeare's use of the unnatural or supernatural to surround the murder of kings or rulers with a special aura of terror. He seems to have associated the idea of unnatural portents with Caesar's death in particular, and returns to it again in HAMLET, a play written immediately after JULIUS CAESAR:

In the most high and palmy state of Rome,
A little ere the mightiest Julius fell,
The graves stood tenantless and the sheeted dead
Did squeak and gibber in the Roman streets;
As stars with trains of fire and dews of blood,
Disaster in the sun; and the moist star
Upon whose influence Neptune's empire stands
Was sick almost to doomsday with eclipse. (I,i,113-)

Shakespeare dwells on these chaotic omens to remind us that Caesar's murder is not simply an individual act of violence. For the Elizabethan audience the overthrow of the ruler or king destroyed also the peace and concord of the state, or society (see Commentary, I,iii). The "fierce fiery warriors,"

To whom it must be done.   331
Caius.   Set on your foot,
And with a heart new-fired I follow you,
To do I know not what; but it sufficeth
That Brutus leads me on.   [*Thunder.*
Brutus.   Follow me then.   [*Exeunt.*

Scene two.

(CAESAR'S HOUSE.)

Thunder and lightning. Enter JULIUS CAESAR, s.d.
in his nightgown.

Caesar. Nor heaven nor earth have been at peace   1
  to-night.
Thrice hath Calpurnia in her sleep cried out
'Help ho! They murder Caesar!' Who's within?   3
      Enter a Servant.
Servant. My lord?
Caesar. Go bid the priests do present sacrifice,   5
And bring me their opinions of success.
Servant. I will, my lord.   [*Exit.*
      Enter CALPURNIA.
Calpurnia. What mean you Caesar? Think you to
  walk forth?
You shall not stir out of your house to-day.
Caesar. Caesar shall forth. The things that threat-
  ened me
Ne'er looked but on my back. When they shall see
The face of Caesar, they are vanished.
Calpurnia. Caesar, I never stood on ceremonies,   13
Yet now they fright me. There is one within,
Besides the things that we have heard and seen,
Recounts most horrid sights seen by the watch.   16
A lioness hath whelped in the streets,
And graves have yawned and yielded up their dead.
Fierce fiery warriors fought upon the clouds
In ranks and squadrons and right form of war,   20
Which drizzled blood upon the Capitol.
The noise of battle hurtled in the air,   22
Horses did neigh, and dying men did groan,
And ghosts did shriek and squeal about the streets.
O Caesar, these things are beyond all use,   25
And I do fear them!
Caesar.   What can be avoided
Whose end is purposed by the mighty gods?
Yet Caesar shall go forth; for these predictions
Are to the world in general as to Caesar.   29
Calpurnia. When beggars die there are no comets
  seen;
The heavens themselves blaze forth the death of
  princes.
Caesar. Cowards die many times before their
  deaths;
The valiant never taste of death but once.
Of all the wonders that I yet have heard,
It seems to me most strange that men should fear,

---

331. "to whom": i.e., and to whom.

Stage Direction "nightgown": dressing-gown.

1. This is heavily ironic; Caesar's "peace" is threatened by another kind of storm.

3. "Who's within": i.e., which of the servants.

5. "priests": who conduct the auguries. "present": immediate.

13. "stood on ceremonies": considered portents of any significance.

16. "watch": watchmen.

20. "right form": battle order.

22. "hurtled": clashed.

25. "use": any usual experience.

29. "Are to": apply as much to.

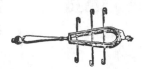

JULIUS CAESAR

ACT II SCENE II

the noise of battle and the groans of dying men (ll. 22-3) are portents suggesting the civil strife and bloody conflict that necessarily (to the Elizabethan mind) followed on the act of rebellion, or the murder of the head of state. Hence these omens and portents of Calpurnia's are important for the whole play as they impress upon us that— despite the integrity of Brutus—what is being planned is bound to produce war and bloodshed. We shall not be surprised at Antony's predictions at III,i,262-275.

Shakespeare's presentation of Caesar in this scene is particularly skillful. He is able to suggest both the self-consciously public figure —the hero to whom fear is unknown—yet also the private individual who yields to his wife's fear (which is also, perhaps, his own). At first Caesar treats the omens as meaningless, and makes them the basis for a typical display of pride: he is "more dangerous" and "elder and more terrible" than danger itself. We are reminded of Cassius' suggestion earlier of Caesar's overweening egotism. Yet as soon as Calpurnia says "Call it my fear" Caesar placates her, and perhaps the actor ought here to suggest another side of Caesar, that we have not seen: not only the Colossus that "bestrides the narrow world," but also a man, here moved by the obvious distress of his wife. However, with the entrance of Decius, Caesar re-asserts the character of the monumental public hero. Unable to make an excuse that might suggest some human weakness he relies on bluster—he is too great to be obliged to explain himself. Calpurnia's interruption ("Say he is sick") is unfortunate in that it forces Caesar to expand on his superiority to the "greybeard" senators. He is now in a perfect position to be undermined by implied threats to this superiority. It is this arrogance that gives Decius his opportunity; he has already told us that he can manipulate Caesar, and now we see this ability at work. There are two things which Caesar's sort of pride cannot stand. One is ridicule, and we note Decius' careful insertion of "lest I be laughed at" at line 70 where the meaning is you and not I. The other is contempt, and Decius, at the end of his speech, is able to suggest that Caesar i) is dependent upon his wife's dreams for his decisions (99), and ii) is, quite simply, afraid (101). Decius gives a masterly performance throughout, particularly in his rapidly improvised interpretation of Calpurnia's dream of Caesar's statue "that did run pure blood." This piece of description (77-9) is, of course, dramatically important since it anticipates for us the actual scene at III,i,76.

Seeing that death, a necessary end,
Will come when it will come.

          Enter a Servant.
             What say the augurers?
  Servant. They would not have you to stir forth
    to-day.
Plucking the entrails of an offering forth,
They could not find a heart within the beast.
  Caesar. The gods do this in shame of cowardice.   41
Caesar should be a beast without a heart   42
If he should stay at home to-day for fear.
No, Caesar shall not. Danger knows full well
That Caesar is more dangerous than he.
We are two lions littered in one day,
And I the elder and more terrible,
And Caesar shall go forth.
  Calpurnia.   Alas, my lord,
Your wisdom is consumed in confidence.   49
Do not go forth to-day. Call it my fear
That keeps you in the house and not your own.
We'll send Mark Antony to the Senate House,
And he shall say you are not well to-day.
Let me upon my knee prevail in this.
  Caesar. Mark Antony shall say I am not well,
And for thy humour I will stay at home.   56
          Enter DECIUS.
Here's Decius Brutus; he shall tell them so.
  Decius. Caesar, all hail! Good morrow, worthy
    Caesar;
I come to fetch you to the Senate House.
  Caesar. And you are come in very happy time   60
To bear my greetings to the senators
And tell them that I will not come to-day.
Cannot, is false; and that I dare not, falser:
I will not come to-day. Tell them so, Decius.
  Calpurnia. Say he is sick.
  Caesar.   Shall Caesar send a lie?
Have I in conquest stretched mine arm so far
To be afeard to tell greybeards the truth?
Decius, go tell them Caesar will not come.
  Decius. Most mighty Caesar, let me know some
    cause,
Lest I be laughed at when I tell them so.   70
  Caesar. The cause is in my will: I will not come.
That is enough to satisfy the Senate;
But for your private satisfaction,
Because I love you, I will let you know.   74
Calpurnia here, my wife, stays me at home.
She dreamt to-night she saw my statue,
Which, like a fountain with an hundred spouts,
Did run pure blood; and many lusty Romans
Came smiling and did bathe their hands in it.
And these does she apply for warnings and portents   80
And evils imminent, and on her knee
Hath begged that I will stay at home to-day.
  Decius. This dream is all amiss interpreted;
It was a vision fair and fortunate.
Your statue spouting blood in many pipes,
In which so many smiling Romans bathed,
Signifies that from you great Rome shall suck
Reviving blood, and that great men shall press

41. "in shame of": i.e., to shame the coward.

42. "Caesar should be": i.e., would himself be.

49. "consumed in": consumed, swallowed by.

56. "humour": feeling (of fear).

60. "very happy time": most opportune time.

70. This line is delivered with the hint of a sneer. Decius must bring Caesar with him.

74. "love you": Plutarch records that Caesar "put such confidence in Decius Brutus, that in his last will and testament he appointed him to be his next heir."

80. "apply": interpret.

39

The conspirators enter, and Caesar orders wine to be prepared for them. This is a subtle touch on Shakespeare's part. We know that Caesar is ambitious, and we know that Brutus honestly believes that he must die for the general good. Yet we have seen him earlier in this scene calming the fears of his wife, and we see him now as a man and a host, offering wine to his murderers. As one of the play's directors has pointed out, the wine has the effect of a "sacrament of trust;" whatever we think of Brutus' integrity, we cannot help but react to the sight of the killers drinking with their unsuspecting victim. Perhaps we recall that, besides Brutus' honesty, the conspiracy comes also from the envy of Cassius, and the mixed motives of the rest (see V,v,69-72). The lines spoken in asides at the end of the scene may also make a distinction between Brutus and the rest of the conspiracy. Trebonius delivers his with something like a snarl of hatred, while Brutus' emotion is, typically, one of sorrow for what he has to do.

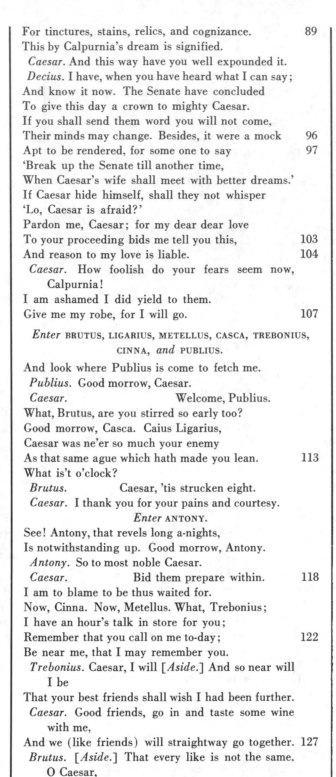

For tinctures, stains, relics, and cognizance. 89
This by Calpurnia's dream is signified.
Caesar. And this way have you well expounded it.
Decius. I have, when you have heard what I can say;
And know it now. The Senate have concluded
To give this day a crown to mighty Caesar.
If you shall send them word you will not come,
Their minds may change. Besides, it were a mock 96
Apt to be rendered, for some one to say 97
'Break up the Senate till another time,
When Caesar's wife shall meet with better dreams.'
If Caesar hide himself, shall they not whisper
'Lo, Caesar is afraid?'
Pardon me, Caesar; for my dear dear love
To your proceeding bids me tell you this, 103
And reason to my love is liable. 104
   Caesar. How foolish do your fears seem now,
     Calpurnia!
I am ashamed I did yield to them.
Give me my robe, for I will go. 107

Enter BRUTUS, LIGARIUS, METELLUS, CASCA, TREBONIUS,
     CINNA, *and* PUBLIUS.

And look where Publius is come to fetch me.
Publius. Good morrow, Caesar.
Caesar.   Welcome, Publius.
What, Brutus, are you stirred so early too?
Good morrow, Casca. Caius Ligarius,
Caesar was ne'er so much your enemy
As that same ague which hath made you lean. 113
What is't o'clock?
Brutus.   Caesar, 'tis strucken eight.
Caesar. I thank you for your pains and courtesy.
     Enter ANTONY.
See! Antony, that revels long a-nights,
Is notwithstanding up. Good morrow, Antony.
Antony. So to most noble Caesar.
Caesar.   Bid them prepare within. 118
I am to blame to be thus waited for.
Now, Cinna. Now, Metellus. What, Trebonius;
I have an hour's talk in store for you;
Remember that you call on me to-day; 122
Be near me, that I may remember you.
   Trebonius. Caesar, I will [*Aside.*] And so near will
     I be
That your best friends shall wish I had been further.
   Caesar. Good friends, go in and taste some wine
     with me,
And we (like friends) will straightway go together. 127
   Brutus. [*Aside.*] That every like is not the same,
     O Caesar,
The heart of Brutus erns to think upon. 129
                   [*Exeunt.*

89. "tinctures": stains or colours used on coats-of-arms.
"relics": remembrances of a saint.
"cognizance": a mark of distinction.

96-7. "mock . . . rendered": i.e., the kind of sarcastic remark one might expect.

103. "proceeding": advancement or career.

104. "reason . . . liable": i.e., my love for you is stronger than my reason (or sense of propriety) in daring to advise you in this way.

107. "robe": the furred Elizabethan robe, or possibly some garment meant to resemble a toga.

113. "ague": fever.

118. "prepare": i.e., the wine.

122. "remember that you": remember to.

127. i.e., both friends and enemies may appear "like" friends.

129. "erns": grieves.

JULIUS CAESAR

ACT II SCENE III

The conspirators are prepared, and their plans are in motion; Decius has persuaded Caesar to go to the Senate. The last two scenes of Act Two provide a kind of bridge passage between the time of Caesar's leaving his house, and his arrival at the Capitol. The characters that appear—Artemidorus in this scene, Portia and the Soothsayer in the next—all have some knowledge or suspicion of the approaching crisis, and they communicate their apprehension to us.

Here Artemidorus has a special function. We have heard a great deal from the anti-Caesar faction in support of the assassination. From Artemidorus we are given an indication of what other Romans might say for and in defence of Caesar. We have no reason to doubt Artemidorus' honesty, and he sees the conflict as between Caesar's "virtue" and the "traitors" who threaten him. This sort of qualification to the view of Caesar as a complete tyrant prevents us from seeing the problem in oversimplifications of good and bad.

ACT II SCENE IV

This scene is based on a brief passage in Plutarch's LIFE OF BRUTUS, and it is interesting to see what Shakespeare makes of it. The passage in Plutarch goes, in part: "Portia was frighted with every noise and cry she heard . . . and sent messenger after messenger, to know what news. Her weakness was not able to hold out any longer, and thereupon she suddenly swooned." Shakespeare's Portia has only one messenger, but she shows her anxiety in her urgent, unthinking demands to Lucius to "run to the Senate house." The short, breathless phrases in lines 13-16 suggest her agitation, verging on incoherence. From Plutarch's "frighted with every noise" Shakespeare imagines the dialogue at lines 16-19. Portia's state is given compressed expression in the line "I heard a bustling rumour like a fray"; "rumour" has the special Elizabethan sense of noise as well as the general meaning of uncertain and possibly dangerous news, and both meanings are present here; they suggest to Portia the word "fray," or battle—her mind moves automatically from any noise she hears to the violence she knows is impending. Shakespeare adds to Plutarch the dialogue between Portia and the Soothsayer. Since he has predicted Caesar's death on this very day, his appearance heightens Portia's anxiety, and our own expectancy. Will he reach Caesar? With the Sooth-

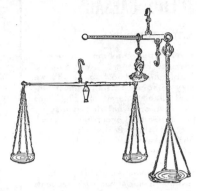

Scene three.

(A STREET.)

Enter ARTEMIDORUS, *reading a paper.*

Artemidorus. 'Caesar, beware of Brutus; take heed of Cassius; come not near Casca; have an eye to Cinna; trust not Trebonius; mark well Metellus Cimber; Decius Brutus loves thee not; thou hast wronged Caius Ligarius. There is but one mind in all these men, and it is bent against Caesar. If thou beest not immortal, look about you. Security gives 7
way to conspiracy. The mighty gods defend thee!

Thy lover,   9
Artemidorus.'

Here will I stand till Caesar pass along
And as a suitor will I give him this. 12
My heart laments that virtue cannot live
Out of the teeth of emulation. 14
If thou read this, O Caesar, thou mayest live;
If not, the Fates with traitors do contrive. [*Exit.* 16

7. "Security": i.e., an unwarranted sense of security.

9. "lover": friend.

12. "suitor": petitioner.

14. "Out . . . emulation": i.e., safe from the bite of envy.

16. "Fates": in classical mythology, the three goddesses who directed human destinies.
"contrive": conspire.

Scene four.

(BEFORE BRUTUS' HOUSE.)

Enter PORTIA *and* LUCIUS.

Portia. I prithee, boy, run to the Senate House.
Stay not to answer me, but get thee gone!
Why dost thou stay?
Lucius.   To know my errand, madam.
Portia. I would have had thee there and here again
Ere I can tell thee what thou shouldst do there.
[*Aside.*] O constancy, be strong upon my side, 6
Set a huge mountain 'tween my heart and tongue!
I have a man's mind, but a woman's might. 8
How hard it is for women to keep counsel! 9
Art thou here yet?
Lucius.   Madam, what should I do?
Run to the Capitol and nothing else?
Portia. Yes, bring me word, boy, if thy lord look
    well,
For he went sickly forth; and take good note
What Caesar doth, what suitors press to him.
Hark, boy! What noise is that?
Lucius. I hear none, madam.
Portia.   Prithee listen well.
I heard a bustling rumour like a fray, 17
And the wind brings it from the Capitol.
Lucius. Sooth, madam, I hear nothing.
    Enter the Soothsayer. s.d.
Portia. Come hither, fellow. Which way hast thou
    been?
Soothsayer. At mine own house, good lady.
Portia. What is't o'clock?
Soothsayer.   About the ninth hour, lady.

6. "constancy": strength, self-control.

8. "might": strength, i.e., a woman's strength.

9. "counsel": secret information. Portia has been told of the plot. That there seems to be no time at which Brutus might have told her is irrelevant. This sort of double time was a convention of the Elizabethan stage, and the difficulty is never noticed during a performance.

17. "bustling rumour": confused noise.

Stage Direction The re-appearance at this point of the Soothsayer who had already warned Caesar of the ides of March (I,ii,18) heightens the tension.

JULIUS CAESAR

ACT II SCENE IV

sayer's apparently innocent remark that the "throng . . . will crowd a feeble man almost to death" we may imagine Portia's almost uncontrollable alarm (ll. 39-43) as she envisions what deaths may be at that moment occurring. Plutarch records that Portia "swooned"; Shakespeare turns this bare fact into dramatic dialogue in Portia's last speech. It is in ironic contrast to her proven ability (II,i,300) to sustain pain on her own account.

ACT III SCENE I

This, the assassination scene, is the central or pivotal scene of the play. All that has gone before leads up to it as a climax, and it provides the motives and impetus for the second half of the play. It is a highly theatrical scene, and we must visualize the action carefully. Caesar enters and moves toward the center of the stage. The Soothsayer and Artemidorus struggle to get near Caesar with their warnings but they are crowded aside, mainly by Decius and Cassius. At the Capitol we have two groups on the stage: Caesar is the center of one, and the conspirators form the other. As the dialogue continues the second group moves slowly to surround and infiltrate the first, loosening the daggers beneath their togas. The tension increases further with Popilius Lena's ambiguous remark to Cassius (l. 13). Shakespeare takes this detail from Plutarch, who goes on to say that the conspirators "were afraid, every man of them, and looked in one another's face," which further suggests to Shakespeare the tense, frightened exchange between Brutus and Cassius (15-22).

Portia. Is Caesar yet gone to the Capitol?

Soothsayer. Madam, not yet. I go take my stand,
To see him pass on to the Capitol.

Portia. Thou hast some suit to Caesar, hast thou not?

Soothsayer. That I have, lady, if it will please Caesar
To be so good to Caesar as to hear me:
I shall beseech him to befriend himself.

Portia. Why, know'st thou any harm's intended towards him?

Soothsayer. None that I know will be, much that I fear may chance.
Good morrow to you. Here the street is narrow.
The throng that follows Caesar at the heels,
Of senators, of praetors, common suitors,
Will crowd a feeble man almost to death.
I'll get me to a place more void and there   36
Speak to great Caesar as he comes along   [*Exit.*

Portia. I must go in. Ay me, how weak a thing
The heart of woman is! O Brutus,
The heavens speed thee in thine enterprise!
Sure the boy heard me.—Brutus hath a suit   41
That Caesar will not grant.—O, I grow faint.—
Run, Lucius, and commend me to my lord;   43
Say I am merry. Come to me again
And bring me word what he doth say to thee.
    [*Exeunt severally.*   s.d.

ACT THREE, scene one.

(ROME. BEFORE THE CAPITOL.)

Flourish. Enter CAESAR, BRUTUS, CASSIUS, CASCA, DECIUS, METELLUS, TREBONIUS, CINNA, ANTONY, LEPIDUS, ARTEMIDORUS, POPILIUS, PUBLIUS *and the* Soothsayer.

Caesar. The ides of March are come.

Soothsayer. Ay, Caesar, but not gone.

Artemidorus. Hail, Caesar! Read this schedule.   3

Decius. Trebonius doth desire you to o'erread
(At your best leisure) this his humble suit.

Artemidorus. O Caesar, read mine first, for mine's a suit
That touches Ceasar nearer. Read it, great Caesar!

Caesar. What touches us ourself shall be last served.

Artemidorus. Delay not, Caesar! Read it instantly!

Caesar. What, is the fellow mad?

Publius.   Sirrah, give place.   10

Cassius. What, urge you your petitions in the street?
Come to the Capitol.

    CAESAR *goes to the Capitol, the rest following.*   s.d.

Popilius. I wish your enterprise to-day may thrive.

Cassius. What enterprise, Popilius?

Popilius.   Fare you well. [*Advances to* CAESAR.

Brutus. What said Popilius Lena?

Cassius. He wished to-day our enterprise might thrive.
I fear our purpose is discovered.

36. "void": empty.

41. "Sure . . . me": Portia suddenly remembers Lucius, who is standing near.

43. "commend me to ": give my wishes for success to.

Stage Direction "severally": by separate entrances at either side of the stage.

3. "schedule": scroll. We know the contents from II,iii.

10. "Sirrah": contemptuous form of address, except when used to a child.

Stage Direction An example of the spatial flexibility of the Elizabethan stage. The audience is to imagine a change of scene at Cassius' "Come to the Capitol." The actors, or Caesar, may go to the recessed inner stage.

JULIUS CAESAR

ACT III SCENE I

Caesar's speeches as the conspirators close in on him (35-48 and 58-74) are in his most arrogant vein. The phrase "preordinance and first decree" which he associates with his own inflexibility are more properly applied to devine or superhuman laws. He is also the "Northern Star," pre-eminent in the heavens, and "Olympus," home of the gods. The suitors surrounding him are, on the other hand, first compared to flatterers given to "Low-crooked curtsies," next to "fawning spaniels" and finally to "curs" whom Caesar kicks aside. The dictator's view of himself as a god has never been more in evidence. A curious detail in the history of Shakespeare criticism is relevant here. Shakespeare's great fellow-dramatist, Ben Jonson, remarked that at this point in the play Shakespeare shows us Caesar replying to a suitor with the line "Caesar never did wrong, but with just cause" which, Jonson adds, was "ridiculous." Jonson's prestige as a critic was great, and presumably it caused Shakespeare to remove the line, since the Folio edition of 1623, on which our texts are based, has instead the lines at 27-8. The substitution is unfortunate; lines 27-8 are weak, and in fact make little sense in the context. Shakespeare's original version (if Jonson recalls it correctly, and there is no reason to doubt him) was far better. Caesar's illogicality, which Jonson presumably objected to, is exactly the sort of thing that a leader, obsessed with his own greatness, and believing himself to be inevitably in the right, might say. It is the dictatorial habit of thought that George Orwell has called "doublethink," and it is quite in accord with everything else Caesar says of himself. Shakespeare, or, as we should prefer to think, the editors of the Folio, have removed a minor but telling detail of characterization from the play.

Returning to our visualization of the action on the stage, we have Caesar elaborating on his own greatness and the conspirators, now grouped tightly around him, in attitudes of supplication. This last detail is important and Shakespeare emphasizes it. Metellus is already on his knees. Cassius, after the beseeching repetition of line 55, falls "as low as to thy foot." Cinna and Decius set up a chorus of "O Caesar, Great Caesar." Their self-abasement is as exaggerated as Caesar's pride. On the stage, this servility will come out even more strongly than in the text, and gives to the audience a sense of ignobility and betrayal that is made emphatic by Casca's movement, as he circles behind Caesar to strike the first blow (see V,i,39-44). Shakespeare again refuses to oversimplify his presen-

---

Brutus. Look how he makes to Caesar. Mark him.

Cassius. Casca, be sudden, for we fear prevention. 19

Brutus, what shall be done? If this be known,

Cassius or Caesar never shall turn back, 21

For I will slay myself.

Brutus.   Cassius, be constant.

Popilius Lena speaks not of our purposes;

For look, he smiles, and Caesar doth not change.

Cassius. Trebonius knows his time, for look you, Brutus,

He draws Mark Antony out of the way

              [*Exeunt* ANTONY *and* TREBONIUS.

Decius. Where is Metellus Cimber? Let him go

And presently prefer his suit to Caesar. 28

Brutus. He is addressed. Press near and second him. 29

Cinna. Casca, you are the first that rears your hand.

Caesar. Are we all ready? What is now amiss

That Caesar and his Senate must redress?

Metellus. Most high, most mighty, and most puissant Caesar,

Metellus Cimber throws before thy seat

An humble heart.   [*Kneels.*

Caesar.   I must prevent thee, Cimber. 35

These couchings, and these lowly courtesies 36

Might fire the blood of ordinary men

And turn preordinance and first decree 38

Into the lane of children. Be not fond 39

To think that Caesar bears such rebel blood 40

That will be thawed from the true quality 41

With that which melteth fools—I mean sweet words,

Low-crooked curtsies, and base spaniel fawning.

Thy brother by decree is banished.

If thou dost bend and pray and fawn for him,

I spurn thee like a cur out of my way.

Know, Caesar doth not wrong, nor without cause

Will he be satisfied.

Metellus.   Is there no voice more worthy than my own,

To sound more sweetly in great Caesar's ear

For the repealing of my banished brother? 51

Brutus. I kiss thy hand, but not in flattery, Caesar,

Desiring thee that Publius Cimber may

Have an immediate freedom of repeal. 54

Caesar. What, Brutus?

Cassius.   Pardon, Caesar! Caesar, pardon!

As low as to thy foot doth Cassius fall

To beg enfranchisement for Publius Cimber.

Caesar. I could be well moved, if I were as you;

If I could pray to move, prayers would move me:

But I am constant as the Northern Star, 60

Of whose true-fixed and resting quality

There is no fellow in the firmament.

The skies are painted with unnumber'd sparks,

They are all fire, and every one doth shine;

But there's but one in all doth hold his place.

So in the world: 'tis furnished well with men,

And men are flesh and blood, and apprehensive; 67

Yet in the number I do know but one

That unassailable holds on his rank, 69

Unshaked of motion; and that I am he,

19. "sudden": quick.

21. "turn back": i.e., return from this alive.

28. "presently prefer": bring at once.

29. "addressed": prepared.

35. "prevent": forestall.

36. "couchings . . . courtesies": grovellings and humble bowing.

38. "turn . . . decree": i.e., change what has been ordained and decreed.

39. "lane": pathway. Some editors print "law".
"fond": so foolish as.

40. "rebel": unstable, unmanageable.

41-6. Shakespeare frequently uses these images of melting, thawing, and the fawning of a dog to express contempt or flattery.

51. "repealing": i.e., repealing the edict which banished his brother.

54. "freedom of repeal": permission to be recalled.

60. "Northern Star": regarded as a symbol of constancy.

67. "apprehensive": capable of reasoning.

69. "holds . . . rank": keeps his position.

JULIUS CAESAR

ACT III SCENE I

tation. Caesar may be a tyrant, but he is also stabbed in the back. The conspirators may be convinced of the rightness of their cause, but cold-blooded murder, operating under the guise of flattery, cannot appear in action as anything but vicious, whatever the reasons. It is said that after Caesar saw Brutus among the conspirators he muffled his head in his toga and ceased to defend himself. On the stage Caesar's recognition of his friend, and the accompanying gesture of hopeless resignation, is particularly effective. We may not be moved to pity for Caesar, but we do recognize the pathos of Brutus, obliged to kill his friend for his principles.

After the assassination, chaos ensues, and we can take the shouts of lines 78-81 to indicate the kind of general noise and movement taking place on the stage. Brutus stands firm in the midst of this. He restrains his followers (82-3), comforts an elderly and frightened senator (85-9), and publicly announces the conspirators' assumption of responsibility for what they have done (94-5). Cassius', ever mindful of the practical, checks on the whereabouts of Antony. In this whirl of talk, of suggestion and counter-suggestion, it becomes clear that the conspirators have no real notion of what it is they do want to do. Even Brutus indicates that whatever develops will be a matter of chance (98). Later we shall be able to compare this undirected enthusiasm to the astute planning of Antony and Octavius.

It is Brutus who suggests the ceremony of washing hands in the blood of Caesar. It is reminiscent of a sacrificial ritual, and we recall the manner in which Brutus earlier viewed the killing (II,i,162-183) as a religious rite, and the conspirators as "purgers" rather than "murderers." Here again Brutus is anxious that others see him (and that he see himself) in a morally acceptable role, performing a duty to the state. However at this point there is, perhaps, some irony in the pretence of the 'religious sacrifice' of Caesar. This will be particularly true on the stage, where the vivid blood provides a silent comment (stage blood was common in the Elizabethan theater). Through Brutus' speech Shakespeare carefully indicates that the conspirators are "Up to the elbows" in blood and wave their "red weapons" over their heads. The bloodstained evidence of murder will make an ironic contrast in the audience's mind with the cries of "Peace, freedom, liberty!"

Let me a little show it, even in this—
That I was constant Cimber should be banished
And constant do remain to keep him so.
Cinna. O Caesar.
Caesar.   Hence! Wilt thou lift up Olympus? 74
Decius. Great Caesar.
Caesar.   Doth not Brutus bootless kneel? 75
Casca. Speak hands for me. [*They stab* CAESAR—
CASCA *first*, BRUTUS *last.*
Caesar. Et tu, Brute?—Then fall Caesar. [*Dies.* 77
Cinna. Liberty! Freedom! Tyranny is dead!
Run hence, proclaim, cry it about the streets!
Cassius. Some to the common pulpits and cry out 80
Liberty, freedom, and enfranchisement!'
Brutus. People and senators, be not affrighted.
Fly not; stand still. Ambition's debt is paid. 83
Casca. Go to the pulpit, Brutus.
Decius.   And Cassius too.
Brutus. Where's Publius? 85
Cinna. Here, quite confounded with the mutiny.
Metellus. Stand fast together, lest some friend of
    Caesar's
Should chance—
Brutus. Talk not of standing! Publius, good cheer.
There is no harm intended to your person
Nor to no Roman else. So tell them, Publius.
Cassius. And leave us, Publius, lest that the people,
Rushing on us, should do your age some mischief.
Brutus. Do so; and let no man abide this deed 94
But we the doers.

Enter TREBONIUS.
Cassius.   Where is Antony?
Trebonius. Fled to his house amazed. 96
Men, wives, and children, stare, cry out, and run,
As it were doomsday.
Brutus.   Fates, we will know your pleasures.
That we shall die, we know; 'tis but the time,
And drawing days out, that men stand upon. 100
Casca. Why, he that cuts off twenty years of life
Cuts off so many years of fearing death.
Brutus. Grant that, and then is death a benefit.
So are we Caesar's friends, that have abridged 104
His time of fearing death. Stoop, Romans, stoop,
And let us bathe our hands in Caesar's blood
Up to the elbows and besmear our swords.
Then walk we forth, even to the market place, 108
And waving our red weapons o'er our heads,
Let's all cry 'Peace, freedom and liberty!'
Cassius. Stoop then and wash. How many ages
    hence
Shall this our lofty scene be acted over
In states unborn and accents yet unknown! 113
Brutus. How many times shall Caesar bleed in sport, 114
That now on Pompey's basis lies along 115
No worthier than the dust!
Cassius.   So oft as that shall be,
So often shall the knot of us be called 117
The men that gave their country liberty.
Decius. What, shall we forth? 119
Cassius.   Ay, every man away.
Brutus shall lead, and we will grace his heels 120

44

---

74. "Olympus": a mountain in Greece, presumed, the home of the gods; Caesar's implication is that he is a god.

75. "bootless": vainly.

77. "Et tu, Brute": the phrase is not in Plutarch, but was conventionally associated with Caesar's assassination.

80. "common pulpits": public platforms.

83. "Ambition's debt": i.e., what Caesar owed to Rome because of his ambition.

85. "Publius": an old senator, whom Brutus singles out to comfort.

FIG. 201.

94. "abide": be responsible for.

96. "amazed": in consternation.

100. "drawing . . . upon": length of life, that men consider important.

104. "abridged": i.e., since we have done Caesar a service in reducing the time during which he might fear death, we are his friends.

108. "market place": The Roman Forum.

113. In Cassius' speech (111-113) predicting the stage performances of Caesar's assassination Shakespeare is, of course, thinking of his own play, performed in the "state unborn and accents yet unknown" (to Cassius) of Elizabethan England. There is, for us, a further pleasant irony that Shakespeare could not forsee, since he could never have predicted the vast popularity and wide dissemination of his work in the four hundred years following his death. What would he have made, for example, of this version of the assassination:
    CAEZAR. ET TU, BRUTE? Basi, anguka Caezar!
    [Anakafu. Wajumbe na raia wanatoka wamepigwa bumbazi.]
    CINNA. Uhuru! Uhuru!
It is taken from a recent translation of the play into Swahili.

114. "in sport": i.e., in the theater.

115. "Pompey's basis": the base of Pompey's statue.

117. "knot": group (of conspirators).

119. "forth": i.e., go forth into the city.

120. "grace his heels": follow him with grace, or honor.

JULIUS CAESAR

ACE III SCENE I

Some critics have seen the entrance of Antony's servant, at line 122, as the turning point of the play. There is no need to try to be exact about the precise point. What is certain is that the arrival of Antony on the scene does change the general movement or direction of the action, since he is the nemesis of the conspirators. The rest of the play is concerned with their defeat and death. Another result of this change in the course of the action is a change in the relationship of the characters. Characters in drama are usually defined by contrast with one another, rather like colors in a painting. Until now there has been a marked contrast between Brutus and Cassius. We have seen a Cassius who is hard-headed, politically astute, a realist who will take any means to further his ends. In all these things he was in sharp contrast to Brutus, whose outstanding characteristics have been (and remain) his high-mindedness, moral concern for the general good of Rome, and a lack of the practical sense and shrewd (and often selfish) judgment needed in a political rebellion. Cassius provided a foil, or contrast to Brutus, and Brutus' character stood out more clearly because of Cassius. With Antony assuming a major role in the play, it is he who provides the contrast to Brutus rather than Cassius. This contrast is most dramatically evident, of course, in the scene containing the two men's funeral orations over Caesar. Cassius, on the other hand, ceases to be contrasted to Brutus in the second half of the play and becomes simply his partner in misfortune.

It is significant that Antony sends his servant to the conspirators before arriving himself. He must make sure the ground is safe, and the servant's speech is a carefully pre-arranged one, in which Antony manages to convey the idea that both Brutus and Caesar are heroes, that he loves them both, and that as he was loyal to Caesar, so will he be able to be loyal to Brutus. What Antony wants is a guarantee of safety until he can put his plans in motion, and this he gets, at once, from Brutus (140-2).

Antony enters almost immediately after his servant, and everything he says in public, from here until the end of his funeral oration, is calculated with extreme cunning to allay suspicion, and give evidence for Brutus' notion that he is straightforward, no schemer, and basically harmless. Cassius has his suspicions, but Antony knows that Brutus is the leader, and it is to Brutus that he directs his performance. First he sets to work on Brutus' well-known honesty and

With the most boldest and best hearts of Rome.
Enter a Servant.
Brutus. Soft! who comes here? A friend of Antony's. 122
Servant. Thus, Brutus, did my master bid me kneel;
Thus did Mark Antony bid me fall down;
And being prostrate, thus he bade me say;
Brutus is noble, wise, valiant, and honest;
Caesar was mighty, bold, royal, and loving.
Say I love Brutus and I honour him;
Say I feared Caesar, honoured him, and loved him.
If Brutus will vouchsafe that Antony 130
May safely come to him and be resolved 131
How Caesar hath deserved to lie in death,
Mark Antony shall not love Caesar dead
So well as Brutus living; but will follow
The fortunes and affairs of noble Brutus
Thorough the hazards of this untrod state 136
With all true faith. So says my master Antony.
Brutus. Thy master is a wise and valiant Roman.
I never thought him worse.
Tell him, so please him come unto this place,
He shall be satisfied and, by my honour,
Depart untouched.
Servant. I'll fetch him presently. [*Exit.*
Brutus. I know that we shall have him well to friend. 143
Cassius. I wish we may. But yet I have a mind
That fears him much; and my misgiving still
Falls shrewdly to the purpose. 146
Enter ANTONY.
Brutus. But here comes Antony. Welcome, Mark Antony.
Antony. O mighty Caesar! dost thou lie so low?
Are all the conquests, glories, triumphs, spoils,
Shrunk to this little measure? Fare thee well.
I know not gentlemen, what you intend,
Who else must be let blood, who else is rank. 152
If I myself, there is no hour so fit
As Caesar's death's hour; nor no instrument
Of half that worth as those your swords, made rich 155
With the most noble blood of all this world.
I do beseech ye, if you bear me hard,
Now, whilst your purpled hands do reek and smoke 158
Fulfil your pleasure. Live a thousand years,
I shall not find myself so apt to die;
No place will please me so, no mean of death, 161
As here by Caesar, and by you cut off,
The choice and master spirits of this age.
Brutus. O Antony, beg not your death of us!
Though now we must appear bloody and cruel,
As by our hands and this our present act
You see we do, yet see you but our hands
And this the bleeding business they have done.
Our hearts you see not. They are pitiful; 169
And pity to the general wrong of Rome
(As fire drives out fire, so pity pity) 171
Hath done this deed on Caesar. For your part,
To you our swords have leaden points, Mark Antony.
Our arms in strength of malice, and our hearts 174
Of brothers' temper do receive you in
With all kind love, good thoughts, and reverence.

122. "Soft!": wait.

130. "vouchsafe": promise.

131. "resolved": satisfied.

136. "Thorough": common Elizabethan form of through.
"untrod state": unknown state of things.

143. "well to friend": as a firm friend.

146. "Falls . . . purpose": is close to the truth.

152. "let blood": purged, as in a therapeutic blood-letting.
"rank": unwholesome, with a pun on too high a rank.

155. "made rich": spoken with as much irony as Antony can here allow himself, as is l. 163.

158. "reek and smoke": i.e., are stained with blood.

161. "mean": method, means.

169. "pitiful": full of pity.

171. The "fire" phrase is proverbial; Brutus means that pity for Rome drove pity for Caesar out of the conspirators' hearts.

174-5. "our . . . in": i.e., both our arms, although they appear hostile, and our hearts, full of brotherly feeling, receive you.

JULIUS CAESAR

ACT III SCENE I

integrity. For Brutus personal betrayal, the desertion of a friend in danger or death would be a moral failing of the first order; therefore Antony begins with a display of grief at the sight of Caesar's body. This is not to say that Antony is being hypocritical. We may assume his deep feeling for Caesar; what is important here is his ability to make tactical use of this feeling. The honest show of grief for the lost friend and the lost cause is exactly the sort of loyalty that will appeal to Brutus. He then does just what Brutus might have done in the same position: offers himself as a victim beside the body of his friend and ruler—"here by Caesar, and by you cut off." It is a shrewd gambit because it forces the conspirators to assure him of his safety, and of their good will toward him —"With all kind love, good thoughts, and reverence." This is Brutus speaking, but notice Cassius' reply to Antony (177-8); Cassius is suspicious of Antony, as one political manipulator of another. He disregards the expressions of grief and loyalty, and makes what is, quite simply, an offer of a share of the proceeds and powers issuing from Caesar's death. Antony, with his eye on the incorruptible Brutus, is careful to overlook this offer.

Antony has not only preserved his life and freedom of action, he has won Brutus' support, and he can now afford to enlarge his role a little. He makes an elaborate show of shaking the hand of each of the assassins in turn. It is not until Act V,i, that the savage irony with which Antony plays his part comes home. The "Gentlemen all" of this speech there become in Antony's words, the murderers who "showed your teeth like apes, and fawned like hounds" and "my valiant Casca" here will there be called "damned Casca" who "like a cur, behind, struck Caesar on the neck."

Antony has one more task—a practical one—and he accomplishes it at lines 227-30. He asks for "reasons" for the killing, and assured by Brutus that he will hear them, he adds another request, as an innocent afterthought—might he "moreover" speak at Caesar's funeral, "as becomes a friend"? And of course Brutus agrees.

Cassius. Your voice shall be as strong as any man's
In the disposing of new dignities.   178
Brutus. Only be patient till we have appeased
The multitude, beside themselves with fear,
And then we will deliver you the cause   181
Why I, that did love Caesar when I struck him,
Have thus proceeded.
Antony.   I doubt not of your wisdom.
Let each man render me his bloody hand.
First, Marcus Brutus, will I shake with you;
Next, Caius Cassius, do I take your hand;
Now, Decius Brutus, yours; now yours, Metellus;
Yours, Cinna; and, my valiant Casca, yours.
Though last, not least in love, yours, good Trebonius.
Gentlemen all—Alas, what shall I say?
My credit now stands on such slippery ground   191
That one of two bad ways you must conceit me,   192
Either a coward or a flatterer.
That I did love thee, Caesar, O, 'tis true!
If then thy spirit look upon us now,
Shall it not grieve thee dearer than thy death
To see thy Antony making his peace,
Shaking the bloody fingers of thy foes,
Most noble! in the presence of thy corse?
Had I as many eyes as thou hast wounds,
Weeping as fast as they stream forth thy blood,
It would become me better than to close   202
In terms of friendship with thine enemies.
Pardon me, Julius! Here wast thou bayed, brave   204
    hart;
Here didst thou fall; and here thy hunters stand,
Signed in thy spoil, and crimsoned in thy lethe.   206
O world, thou wast the forest to this hart;
And this indeed, O world, the heart of thee!
How like a deer, stroken by many princes,   209
Dost thou here lie!
Cassius. Mark Antony—
Antony.   Pardon me, Caius Cassius.
The enemies of Caesar shall say this: 212
Then, in a friend, it is cold modesty.
Cassius. I blame you not for praising Caesar so;
But what compact mean you to have with us?
Will you be pricked in number of our friends,   216
Or shall we on, and not depend on you?
Antony. Therefore I took your hands, but was indeed
Swayed from the point by looking down on Caesar.
Friends am I with you all, and love you all,
Upon this hope, that you shall give me reasons
Why and wherein Caesar was dangerous.
Brutus. Or else were this a savage spectacle.
Our reasons are so full of good regard   224
There were you, Antony, the son of Caesar,
You should be satisfied.
Antony.   That's all I seek;
And am moreover suitor that I may   227
Produce his body to the market place
And in the pulpit, as becomes a friend,
Speak in the order of his funeral.   230
Brutus. You shall, Mark Antony.
Cassius.   Brutus, a word with you.

178. "dignities": honors and offices of state.

181. "deliver": explain at length.

191. "credit": i.e., the trust others may have in me.

192. "conceit": think of, consider.

202. "become me better": suit me better, i.e., as Caesar's friend. "close": make an agreement with.

204. "bayed": brought to bay. "hart": deer, with a pun on heart.

206. "Signed . . . spoil": i.e., smeared with the blood of thy slaughter. Technically "spoil" refers to those parts of the hunted animal which were distributed to the hounds. "lethe": in classical mythology Lethe was a river in Hades, the waters of which induced forgetfulness. Here the association is with death generally.

209. "stroken": struck.

212-13. "enemies . . . modesty": i.e., even Caesar's enemies would say as much as this; therefore, it is moderate in a friend.

216. "pricked": marked on a list.

224. "regard": considerations.

227. "And . . . suitor": i.e., and now I ask.

230. "order": ceremony.

JULIUS CAESAR

ACT III SCENE I

In the ensuing debate between Cassius and Brutus (held in asides, 232-243) it is clear that Cassius is still the practical thinker of the conspiracy but that Brutus, the moral mainstay and public leader, can overrule him (as he does also at II,i,50 ff.). Brutus' argument here is interesting because it reveals both his lack of astuteness as far as other people are concerned—after Antony's honest performance, he refuses to suspect him—and his naive certainty that his own cause, because it is right, need only be put to the people to convince them. "I will myself into the pulpit first / And show the reason of our Caesar's death" seems to him a sufficient answer to Cassius' doubts.

The conspirators leave the stage to Antony, and his violent, sulphuric outburst gives some indication of the strain under which he has been laboring. With them his language had been careful and controlled in accordance with the effects he wished to produce. Here we have naked, undisguised grief, hatred, and an impassioned desire for revenge. The "gentlemen" become "these butchers," and Antony moves on from them to the notion of the general carnage which will result from Caesar's death. The ghost seeking revenge was a familiar and sinister figure on the Elizabethan stage, and Antony conjures it up here for the audience with "Caesar's spirit, ranging for revenge . . . come hot from hell." But this is more than a figure of speech, or reference to the stage convention of the revenger. There are, in fact, two Caesar's in the play: the man the conspirators have killed, and the "spirit" who haunts the rest of the play, and whose effect we shall see in Acts IV and V. Antony's speech here, with its predictions concerning "Domestic fury and fierce civil strife" attest to the power of this second Caesar. Shakespeare also solves a technical

[*Aside to Brutus.*] You know not what you do. Do
   not consent
That Antony speak in his funeral.
Know you how much the people may be moved
By that which he will utter?
   Brutus. [*Aside to Cassius.*] By your pardon—
I will myself into the pulpit first
And show the reasons for our Caesar's death.
What Antony shall speak, I will protest   238
He speaks by leave and by permission;
And that we are contented Caesar shall
Have all true rites and lawful ceremonies.
It shall advantage more than do us wrong.   242
   Cassius. [*Aside to Brutus.*] I know not what may
     fall. I like it not.
   Brutus. Mark Antony, here, take your Caesar's body
You shall not in your funeral speech blame us,
But speak all good you can devise of Caesar;
And say you do't by our permission.
Else shall you not have any hand at all
About his funeral. And you shall speak
In the same pulpit whereto I am going,
After my speech is ended.
   Antony.   Be it so.
I do desire no more.
   Brutus. Prepare the body then, and follow us.
               [*Exeunt all except* ANTONY
   Antony. O, pardon me, thou bleeding piece of earth,
That I am meek and gentle with these butchers!
Thou art the ruins of the noblest man
That ever lived in the tide of times.   257
Woe to the hand that shed this costly blood!
Over thy wounds now do I prophesy
(Which, like dumb mouths, do ope their ruby lips
To beg the voice and utterance of my tongue),
A curse shall light upon the limbs of men;
Domestic fury and fierce civil strife   263
Shall cumber all the parts of Italy;   264
Blood and destruction shall be so in use   265
And dreadful objects so familiar
That mothers shall but smile when they behold
Their infants quartered with the hands of war,   268
All pity choked with custom of fell deeds   269
And Caesar's spirit, ranging for revenge,   270
With Ate by his side come hot from hell,   271
Shall in these confines with a monarch's voice 272
Cry 'Havoc!' and let slip the dogs of war,   273
That this foul deed shall smell above the earth
With carrion men, groaning for burial.   275
           Enter OCTAVIUS' *servant.*
You serve Octavius Caesar, do you not?
   Servant. I do, Mark Antony.
   Antony. Caesar did write for him to come to Rome.
   Servant. He did receive his letters and is coming,
And bid me say to you by word of mouth—
O Caesar!
   Antony. Thy heart is big. Get thee apart and weep.
Passion, I see, is catching; for mine eyes,   283
Seeing those beads of sorrow stand in thine,
Began to water. Is thy master coming?

238. "protest": announce.

242. "advantage": benefit.

257. "tide of times": stream of time, or history.

263. "Domestic": internal.

264. "cumber": burden.

265. "so in use": so common.

268. "quartered": cut in pieces.

269. "custom . . . deeds": familiarity with cruel deeds.

270. "ranging": hunting.

271. "Ate": classical goddess of destruction.

272. "confines": localities.

273. "Cry 'Havoc'": the signal, given by the commander of a victorious army, for the total destruction of the enemy.
"let slip": unleash.

275. "carrion men": decaying corpses.

283. "Passion": here, grief.

JULIUS CAESAR

ACT III SCENE I

dramatic problem with Antony's speech. Through the play thus far our concentration has been on the events leading to the murder of Caesar. Now that Caesar is dead there would be an inevitable relaxation in dramatic pressure, were it not for the force of Antony's speech here, and its anticipation of new crises to come. Of course in the theater we would never realize that Shakespeare had 'a dramatic problem' at this point, simply because he solves it so deftly.

ACT III SCENE II

In this scene Antony's power is made clear, and it is a power which works, not through physical violence, but verbal persuasion. This point is important to the play as a whole. JULIUS CAESAR is a political play in the broadest sense of that term: it deals with the way men achieve power, and the attempt to justify their actions to others, and to society. A large part of the first half of the play is concerned with persuasion, the ways in which people can be convinced, by honest or dishonest argument, that they ought to act in a certain way. Notice how many occasions we have had, up to this point, to watch people being 'talked into' something. The tribunes convince the people that they ought not to celebrate Caesar's triumph; Cassius convinces Brutus that Caesar ought to be destroyed; Portia convinces Brutus that he ought to tell her of his plans; Calpurnia convinces Caesar that he ought not to go to the Capitol, and Decius convinces him that he must go. This scene is wholly constructed of two opposing arguments: Brutus' defence of Caesar's assassination, and Antony's attack on it. The scene is important not simply because of its importance to the plot, but because it also deals with one of the main issues, or questions, of the play—how do people act, when confronted with a vital public or political decision? On the basis of this scene the answer is that their actions are far from rational, and that they can be directed at will by anyone who, like Antony, can manipulate an audience with his words.

The funeral speech, or LAUDATIO FUNEBRIS, was a common Roman custom, Plutarch mentions it in connection with Caesar's death, but he gives no account of what was said. Shakespeare invents both speeches, and makes them into a brilliant contrast.

Servant. He lies to-night within seven leagues of Rome.

Antony. Post back with speed and tell him what hath chanced. 287
Here is a mourning Rome, a dangerous Rome,
No Rome of safety for Octavius yet.
Hie hence and tell him so. Yet stay awhile.
Thou shalt not back till I have born this corse
Into the market place. There shall I try 292
In my oration how the people take
The cruel issue of these bloody men; 294
According to the which thou shalt discourse
To young Octavius of the state of things.
Lend me your hand   [*Exeunt with* CAESAR's *body.*

Scene two.

(THE FORUM)

Enter BRUTUS *and goes into the pulpit, and* CASSIUS *and the citizens.*

Citizens. We will be satisfied! Let us be satisfied! 1
Brutus. Then follow me and give me audience, friends.
Cassius, go you into the other street
And part the numbers. 4
Those that will hear me speak, let 'em stay here;
Those that will follow Cassius, go with him;
And public reasons shall be rendered 7
Of Caesar's death.
1st Citizen.   I will hear Brutus speak.
2nd Citizen. I will hear Cassius, and compare their reasons
When severally we hear them rendered. 10
3d Citizen. The noble Brutus is ascended. Silence!
Brutus. Be patient till the last.
Romans, countrymen, and lovers, hear me for my 13
cause, and be silent, that you may hear. Believe
me for mine honour, and have respect to mine hon- 15
our, that you may believe. Censure me in your 16
wisdom and awake your senses, that you may the
better judge. If there be any in this assembly, any
dear friend of Caesar's, to him I say that Brutus'
love to Caesar was no less than his. If then that
friend demand why Brutus rose against Caesar,
this is my answer: Not that I loved Caesar less,
but that I loved Rome more. Had you rather Caesar
were living, and die all slaves, than that Caesar
were dead, to live all freemen? As Caesar loved
me, I weep for him; as he was fortunate, I rejoice
at it; as he was valiant, I honour him; but—
as he was ambitious, I slew him. There is tears for
his love; joy for his fortune; honour for his valour;
and death for his ambition. Who is here so base that
would be a bondman? If any, speak; for him I have 31
offended. Who is here so rude that would not be a 32
Roman? If any, speak; for him have I offended.
Who is here so vile that will not love his country? If

---

287. "chanced": happened.

292. "try": test.

294. "cruel issue": the result of the cruelty.

1. "will be satisfied": have a full explanation.

4. "part the numbers": divide the people.

7. "public reasons": i) reasons for the public to hear, or ii) reasons having to do with the public good.

10. "severally": separately.

13. "lovers": dear friends.

15. "have respect to": remember.

16. "Censure": judge.

31. "bondman": slave.

32. "rude": uncivilized, barbaric.

JULIUS CAESAR

ACT III SCENE II

Everything about the two speakers —their characters, political attitudes, strengths and weaknesses— is implicitly present in what they say.

Brutus speaks in prose, a form which suits the sober, orderly presentation of what he has to say. His calm prosaic, and colorless delivery is in direct contrast with the poetry of Antony. Brutus' opening remarks ("Be patient to the last . . . be silent, that you may hear") have the quality of a teacher rapping for the attention of his class, and what he says is very like a lecture. The construction of the speech is careful and controlled. Notice, for example, the continual use of parallel constructions from line 25 on (e.g., loved-weep, fortunate-rejoice, valiant-honour, ambitious- slew). This sort of arrangement has the effect of rational, logical development, almost like a mathematical demonstration, and Brutus' "I pause for a reply" at the end of the passage is a confident "Q.E.D." Brutus has made two vital errors of judgment in this speech, and both of them stem (as all his errors do) from qualities in him which we admire. In the first place he has assumed that, since his cause is just, it needs only to be presented to be believed. It is one of his fundamental beliefs that justice and truth will prevail in this world, and it is shown to be a naive one. His second mistake is to assume that others, like himself, will be persuaded by reason. The qualities of the crowd that Antony works on so effectively—emotion, fuzzy-mindedness, greed—are incomprehensible to Brutus. One of the great defects of his virtue is to assume the existence of the same virtue in everyone else. Brutus' dangerous lack of insight into the practical realities of persuasion and the mob-mind is further revealed in his complete misunderstanding of the reaction to his speech. He has demonstrated with clarity and precision why the death of Caesar, or of any tyrant who wants to 'be a Caesar,' is necessary. The crowd's acclaim shows how little they have understood him. The shout of "Let him be Caesar" is an effective comment on their ignorance of the real issues involved. Yet Brutus does not see that a crowd which can acclaim him for all the wrong reasons is also one which can be totally reworked by Antony. Innocently confident of the justice and success of his own cause, Brutus leaves the speaking platform to his adversary.

any, speak; for him I have offended. I pause for a reply.

All. None, Brutus, none!

Brutus. Then none have I offended. I have done no more to Caesar than you shall do to Brutus. The question of his death is enrolled in the Capitol; his 40 glory not extenuated, wherein he was worthy; nor 41 his offenses enforced, for which he suffered death. 42

Enter MARK ANTONY *and others, with* CAESAR'S *body.*

Here comes his body, mourned by Mark Antony, who, though he had no hand in his death, shall receive the benefit of his dying, a place in the com- 45 monwealth, as which of you shall not? With this I depart, that, as I slew my best lover for the good 47 of Rome, I have the same dagger for myself when it shall please my country to need my death.

All. Live, Brutus! Live, live!

1st Citizen. Bring him with triumph home unto his house.

2nd Citizen. Give him a statue with his ancestors.

3d Citizen. Let him be Caesar.

4th Citizen. Caesar's better parts Shall be crowned in Brutus.

1st Citizen. We'll bring him to his house with shouts and clamours.

Brutus. My countrymen—

2nd Citizen. Peace! Silence! Brutus speaks,

1st Citizen. Peace, ho!

Brutus. Good countrymen, let me depart alone, And for my sake, stay here with Antony. Do grace to Caesar's corse, and grace his speech 60 Tending to Caesar's glories which Mark Antony, By our permission, is allowed to make. I do entreat you, not a man depart, Save I alone, till Antony have spoke. [*Exit.*

1st Citizen. Stay, ho! and let us hear Mark Antony.

3rd Citizen. Let him go up into the public chair. We'll hear him, noble Antony, go up.

Antony. For Brutus sake I am beholding to you. 68
[ANTONY *goes into the pulpit.*

4th Citizen. What does he say of Brutus?

3d Citizen. He says for Brutus' sake He finds himself beholding to us all.

4th Citizen. 'Twere best he speak no harm of Brutus here!

1st Citizen. This Caesar was a tyrant.

3d Citizen. Nay, that's certain. We are blest that Rome is rid of him.

2nd Citizen. Peace! Let us hear what Antony can say.

Antony. You gentle Romans—

All. Peace, ho! Let us hear him.

Antony. Friends, Romans, countrymen, lend me your ears; I come to bury Caesar, not to praise him. The evil that men do lives after them; The good is oft interred with their bones. So let it be with Caesar. The noble Brutus Hath told you Caesar was ambitious. If it were so, it was a grievous fault, And grievously hath Caesar answered it. 83

40. "enrolled": officially recorded.

41. "extenuated": understated.

42. "enforced": overstated.

45. "place": i.e., as a free citizen.

47. "lover": friend.

60. "grace": i.e., treat with respect both Caesar's body, and the speech which Antony is about to make.

68. "beholding": indebted.

83. "answered it": paid the penalty for it.

JULIUS CAESAR

ACT III SCENE II

Antony's speech has been generally considered one of Shakespeare's most brilliant creations. Sir Harley Granville-Barker comments: "The cheapening of the truth, the appeals to passion, the perfect carillon of flattery, cajolery, mockery and pathos, swinging to a magnificent tune, all serve to make it a model of what popular oratory should be. In a school for demagogues its critical analysis might well be an item on every examination paper." In fact Antony's demagoguery is such that audiences are often taken in by it. As in the preceding scene, Antony's emotion is genuine; it is the subtle manipulation of the audience which lies beneath the apparent artlessness of the speech that is so clever.

When Antony takes the stand his audience is clearly pro-Brutus (68) and he guides himself accordingly. He disavows any intention of praising Caesar, and refers to the "noble" Brutus. There is, however, the thin end of the wedge at the mention of Caesar's ambition—"If it were so"—at line 82. Antony is careful not to proceed too rapidly, and the phrase "honourable man" (85) is delivered as a straightforward phrase. The word "honourable" recurs in the speech like a refrain. It is used eight times, each time with increasing bitterness, and finally in open contempt. Actors who play Antony often make the mistake of making Antony say the word sarcastically at the very outset of the speech; but Antony waits until the crowd is itself ready to give the word a savage inflection—"They were traitors. Honourable men!"

Antony's operation on his hearers falls into several phases. First he deals with the question of Caesar's ambition, carefully slanting his remarks so they will appeal to i) the people's poverty—Caesar filled the "general coffers," and "wept" when the poor were unhappy, and ii) their sense of their own importance: they would all recall that it was at their insistence that Caesar refused the crown offered to him at the feast of Lupercal. Next, Antony suggests that, in refusing to mourn Caesar, "men have lost their reason." This may be too directly critical at this stage, so he shifts their attention with a display of his own emotion (108-10). Antony's point is made. The citizens see that "there is much reason" in what he says (heavily ironic, when one remembers the genuinely reasonable speech by Brutus) and are also affected by his grief (118). Next Antony uses the rhetorical device of introducing an idea which he wishes his audience to take up by pretending to disclaim it. To move the crowd "to mutiny and rage" would be to

Here under leave of Brutus and the rest
(For Brutus is an honourable man;
So are they all, all honourable men),
Come I to speak in Caesar's funeral.
He was my friend, faithful and just to me;
But Brutus says he was ambitious,
And Brutus is an honourable man.
He hath brought many captives home to Rome,
Whose ransoms did the general coffers fill.   92
Did this in Caesar seem ambitious?
When that the poor have cried, Caesar hath wept;
Ambition should be made of sterner stuff.
Yet Brutus says he was ambitious;
And Brutus is an honourable man.
You all did see that on the Lupercal
I thrice presented him a kingly crown,
Which he did thrice refuse. Was this ambition?
Yet Brutus says he was ambitious;
And sure he is an honourable man.
I speak not to disprove what Brutus spoke,
But here I am to speak what I do know.
You all did love him once, not without cause.
What cause withholds you then to mourn for him?
O judgment, thou art fled to brutish beasts,
And men have lost their reason! Bear with me.
My heart is in the coffin there with Caesar,
And I must pause till it come back to me.

1st Citizen. Methinks there is much reason in his
   sayings.
2nd Citizen. If thou consider rightly of the matter,
Caesar has had great wrong.
3d Citizen.   Has he, masters?
I fear there will a worse come in his place.
4th Citizen. Marked ye his words? He would not
   take the crown;
Therefore 'tis certain he was not ambitious.
1st Citizen. If it be found so, some will dear abide it.   117
2nd Citizen. Poor soul! His eyes are red as fire
   with weeping.
3d Citizen. There's not a nobler man in Rome than
   Antony.
4th Citizen. Now mark him. He begins again to
   speak.
Antony. But yesterday the word of Caesar might
Have stood against the world. Now lies he there,
And none so poor to do him reverence   123
O masters! If I were disposed to stir
Your hearts and minds to mutiny and rage,
I should do Brutus wrong, and Cassius wrong,
Who, you all know, are honourable men.
I will not do them wrong. I rather choose
To wrong the dead, to wrong myself and you,
Than I will wrong such honourable men.
But here's a parchment with the seal of Caesar.
I found it in his closet; 'tis his will.
Let but the commons hear this testament,   133
Which (pardon me) I do not mean to read,
And they would go and kiss dead Caesar's wounds
And dip their napkins in his sacred blood;   136
Yea, beg a hair of him for memory,
And dying, mention it within their wills,

92. "general coffers": public treasuries.

117. "dear abide it": pay heavily for it.

123. "none so poor": none humble enough. Antony speaks with heavy irony here—apparently you are too great to show reverence for Caesar.

133. "commons": ordinary citizens. "testament": will.

136. "napkins": handkerchiefs.

do wrong to the conspirators, and he would rather "wrong the dead . . . and you." It is a subtle touch, and suggests to the listeners that they are on Caesar's side, that they have been wronged, and that "mutiny and rage" may be in order. Thus far Antony has used innuendo and implication; it is time for something tangible and solid, and he introduces Caesar's will. Where a less skillful orator would certainly proceed, at this climax, to capitalize on the introduction of the will by reading it, Antony holds back. Instead he works on his audience's boundless suggestibility by telling them what they will feel when they do hear it, unless they are "wood" or "stones." Now Antony descends to Caesar's body; by this point he is in complete control, and he orders and arranges the crowd at will (169). It is time for more tangible evidence, now of a direct and visual kind, and Antony indicates the blood-stained "rants" in Caesar's toga, ending with the wound inflicted by "well-beloved" Brutus. Antony can now risk open incitement to violence against the "blood treason" he has revealed. Were he an able speaker, he says (with an irony lost on his hearers), he would move "The stones of Rome to rise and mutiny." This is enough for the mob, but as they set off to find the conspirators, Antony calls them back. He has worked his will on them, and he can now afford to point out with something close to amused contempt (which they of course miss) the senselessness of the passions he has aroused—"you go to do you know not what." They have forgotten the will. Antony is astute enough to know that while a group will act violently and immediately on the basis of a powerful shared emotion, something further is needed to motivate the individual when the group-emotion has passed. Therefore he ends his incitement with a specific appeal to the greed of each of them—Caesar's bequest of the "walks, arbors, orchards" and to "every several man, seventy-five drachmas." And only then is he content to let them go.

Bequeathing it as a rich legacy
Unto their issue.
   4th Citizen. We'll hear the will! Read it, Mark
     Antony.
   All. The will, the will! We will hear Caesar's will!
   Antony. Have patience, gentle friends; I must not
     read it.
It is not meet you know how Caesar loved you.   144
You are not wood, you are not stones, but men;
And being men, hearing the will of Caesar,
It will inflame you, it will make you mad.
'Tis good you know not that you are his heirs;
For if you should, O, what would come of it?
   4th Citizen. Read the will! We'll hear it, Antony!
You shall read us the will, Caesar's will!
   Antony. Will you be patient? Will you stay awhile?
I have o'ershot myself to tell you of it.
I fear I wrong the honourable men
Whose daggers have stabbed Caesar; I do fear it.
   4th Citizen. They were traitors. Honourable men!
   All. The will! The testament!
   2nd Citizen. They were villains, murderers! The
     will! Read the will!
   Antony. You will compel me then to read the will?
Then make a ring about the corse of Caesar
And let me show you him that made the will.
Shall I descend? and will you give me leave?
   All. Come down.
   2nd Citizen. Descend.
   3d Citizen. You shall have leave.
             [ANTONY *comes down.*
   4th Citizen. A ring! Stand round.
   1st Citizen. Stand from the hearse! Stand from   167
     the body!
   2nd Citizen. Room for Antony, most noble Antony!
   Antony. Nay, press not so upon me. Stand far off.
   All. Stand back! Room! Bear back!
   Antony. If you have tears, prepare to shed them now.
You all do know this mantle. I remember   172
The first time ever Caesar put it on.
'Twas on a summer's evening in his tent,
That day he overcame the Nervii.   175
Look, in this place ran Cassius' dagger through.
See what a rent the envious Casca made.
Through this the well beloved Brutus stabbed;
And as he plucked his cursed steel away,
Mark how the blood of Caesar followed it,
As rushing out of doors to be resolved   181
If Brutus so unkindly knocked or no;
For Brutus, as you know, was Caesar's angel.   183
Judge, O you gods, how dearly Caesar loved him!
This was the most unkindest cut of all;   185
For when the noble Caesar saw him stab,
Ingratitude, more strong than traitors' arms,
Quite vanquished him. Then burst his mighty heart;
And in his mantle muffling up his face,
Even at the base of Pompey's statue
(Which all the while ran blood) great Caesar fell.
O what a fall was there, my countrymen!
Then I, and you, and all of us fell down,
Whilst bloody treason flourished over us.

144. "meet": proper, right.

167. "hearse": bier.

172. "mantle": toga.

175. "Nervii": a tribe defeated by the Romans in Caesar's Gallic wars.

181. "to be resolved": to make certain.

183. "angel": most favored companion.

185. "most unkindest": most unnatural; an emphatic double superlative.

51

O, now you weep, and I perceive you feel
The dint of pity. These are gracious drops.   196
Kind souls, what weep you when you but behold
Our Caesar's vesture wounded? Look you here!
Here is himself, marred as you see with traitors.   199
  1st Citizen. O piteous spectacle!
  2nd Citizen. O noble Caesar!
  3d Citizen. O woeful day!
  4th Citizen. O traitors, villains!
  1st Citizen. O most bloody sight!
  2nd Citizen. We will be revenged.
  All. Revenge! About! Sneak! Burn! Fire! Kill!
    Slay!
Let not a traitor live!
  Antony. Stay, countrymen.
  1st Citizen. Peace there! Hear the noble Antony.
  2nd Citizen. We'll hear him, we'll follow him, we'll
    die with him!
  Antony. Good friends, sweet friends, let me not
    stir you up
To such a sudden flood of mutiny.
They that have done this deed are honourable.
What private griefs they have, alas, I know not,   214
That made them do it. They are wise and honourable,
And will no doubt with reasons answer you.
I came not, friends, to steal away your hearts.
I am no orator, as Brutus is,
But (as you know me all) a plain blunt man
That love my friend; and that they know full well
That gave me public leave to speak of him.   221
For I have neither writ, nor words, nor worth,   222
Action, nor utterance, nor the power of speech   223
To stir men's blood. I only speak right on.
I tell you that which you yourselves do know,
Show you sweet Caesar's wounds, poor poor dumb
    mouths,
And bid them speak for me. But were I Brutus,
And Brutus Antony, there were an Antony
Would ruffle up your spirits, and put a tongue   229
In every wound of Caesar that should move
The stones of Rome to rise and mutiny.
  All. We'll mutiny.
  1st Citizen.   We'll burn the house of Brutus.
  3d Citizen. Away then! Come, seek the conspirators.
  Antony. Yet hear me, countrymen. Yet hear me
    speak.
  All. Peace, ho! Hear Antony, most noble Antony!
  Antony. Why friends, you go to do you know not
    what.
Wherein hath Caesar thus deserved your loves?
Alas, you know not! I must tell you then.
You have forgot the will I told you of.
  All. Most true! The will! Let's stay and hear the
    will.
  Antony. Here is the will, and under Caesar's seal.
To every Roman citizen he gives,
To every several man, seventy-five drachmas.   243
  2nd Citizen. Most noble Caesar! We'll revenge his
    death.
  3d Citizen. O royal Caesar!
  Antony. Hear me with patience.

196. "dint": impression, as in dent.
"gracious'" full of grace, honorable.

199. "marred": mutilated.

214. "private griefs": personal grievances. Antony suggests that there may be some.

221. "public . . . speak": leave to speak in public.

222. "writ": a speech prepared, or written out. Many editors print wit.

223. "Action": use of gesture.
"utterance": verbal delivery.

229. "ruffle up": raise in anger, as a dog's ruff.

243. "seventy-five drachmas": Today, about $30.

The purpose of this scene is to dramatize, in one brief, violent incident, the result of Antony's oratory. The first act of the mob, their emotions inflamed and their reason obscured, is the senseless murder of an innocent man. The mob mistakes Cinna the poet for Cinna the conspirator; yet even when he tells them their mistake, they butcher him anyway "for his bad verses." There is a curious irony in the fact that the man whose life was devoted to the perceptive and sensitive use of language should be the victim of a totally different way of using language—to produce rage, hatred, and destructive hysteria.

Shakespeare's handling of this mob scene and some others like it (notably in CORIOLANUS) has caused some critics to say that he distrusted and even hated, the ordinary people. This judgment is based on a misunderstanding of the way Shakespeare treats 'the people' in his plays. In this play, for example, we are given a group of "commoners" in the opening scene, but they are not a 'mob.'

All. Peace, ho!
Antony. Moreover he hath left you all his walks,   248
His private arbors, and new-planted orchards,
On this side Tiber; he hath left them you,
And to your heirs for ever—common pleasures,
To walk abroad and recreate yourselves.
Here was a Caesar! When comes such another?
1st Citizen. Never, never! Come away, away!
We'll burn his body in the holy place   255
And with the brands fire the traitors' houses.
Take up the body.
2nd Citizen. Go fetch fire!
3d Citizen. Pluck down benches!
4th Citizen. Pluck down forms, windows, anything! 260
      [*Exit citizens with the body.*
Antony. Now let it work. Mischief, thou art afoot,
Take thou what course thou wilt.
      Enter servant.
      How now, fellow?
Servant. Sir, Octavia is already come to Rome.
Antony. Where is he?
Servant. He and Lepidus are at Caesar's house.
Antony. And thither will I straight to visit him.
He comes upon a wish. Fortune is merry,   267
And in this mood will give us anything.
Servant. I heard him say Brutus and Cassius
Are rid like madmen through the gates of Rome.   270
Antony. Belike they had some notice of the people, 271
How I had moved them. Bring me to Octavius.
      [*Exeunt.*

Scene three.

(ROME. A STREET)

Enter CINNA, *the Poet, and after him the citizens.*
Cinna. I dreamt to-night that I did feast with   1
    Caesar,
And things unluckily charge my fantasy.   2
I have no will to wander forth of doors,
Yet something leads me forth.
1st Citizen. What is your name?
2nd Citizen. Whither are you going?
3d Citizen. Where do you dwell?
4th Citizen. Are you a married man or a bachelor?
2nd Citizen. Answer every man directly.
1st Citizen. Ay, and briefly.
4th Citizen. Ay, and wisely.
3d Citizen. Ay, and truly, you were best.
Cinna. What is my name? Whither am I going?
Where do I dwell? Am I a married man or a
bachelor? Then, to answer every man directly and
briefly, wisely and truly: wisely I say, I am a
bachelor.
2nd Citizen. That's as much as to say they are
fools that marry. You'll bear me a bang for that,   19
I fear. Proceed directly.
Cinna. Directly I am going to Caesar's funeral.

248. "his walks": see note at I,ii,155.

255. "the holy place": among the sacred temples of Rome.

260. "windows": shutters.

267. "upon a wish": just as I wished it.

270. "Are rid": have ridden.

271. "notice": news. This comes from Antony as a grim understatement.

1. "to-night": last night.

2. "things . . . fantasy": i.e., what has happened to Caesar makes me imagine I may share his fate ("feast").

19. "bear me a bang": get a beating from me.

JULIUS CAESAR

ACT III SCENE III

They are rather a collection of individuals—carpenters and cobblers and so on—and indeed they contain the only comic role in the play, the amiable cobbler who outwits the tribunes. If we compare them to the crowd in III,ii, and iii, we see the difference. In the latter scenes there are no individuals, only a mob, swayed by mob-emotions. What they say is neither individual, or witty, as in the case of the cobbler, but a generalized, undifferentiated shout of violence —"Tear him, tear him! Come, brands ho! firebrands!" We meet a great many 'ordinary people' in Shakespeare—bright and stupid, sweet and sour, proper and improper—and they are all, in their way, attractive. But we never meet an attractive mob.

ACT IV SCENE I

In III,iii, we witnessed the public result of Antony's victory—mindless brutality. In this scene we are shown the result at a higher political level—the deliberate, cold-blooded imposition of the death sentence on a long list of Romans. Plutarch's version is as follows: "They could hardly agree whom they would put to death: for every one of them would kill their enemies and save their kinsmen and friends. Yet at length, giving place to their greedy desire to be revenged of their enemies, they spurned all reverence of blood and holiness of friendship at their feet . . . they condemned three hundred of the chiefest citizens of Rome to be put to death by proscription."

Antony's opening line, which is particularly effective because of the contrast between its flat, unemotional tone and its subject, sets the tone. There follows a grisly piece of relative-trading between Antony and Lepidus (2-6), and then Antony's announcement that he has no intention (and possibly never did have any intention) of fulfilling the promises in Caesar's will which he had used so effectively to enrage the mob against the conspirators. Although he is

---

1st Citizen. As a friend or an enemy?

Cinna. As a friend.

2nd Citizen. That matter is answered directly.

4th Citizen. For your dwelling—briefly.

Cinna. Briefly, I dwell by the Capitol.

3d Citizen. Your name, sir, truly.

Cinna. Truly, my name is Cinna.

1st Citizen. Tear him to pieces! He's a conspirator.

Cinna. I am Cinna the poet! I am Cinna the poet!

4th Citizen. Tear him for his bad verses! Tear him for his bad verses!

Cinna. I am not Cinna the conspirator.

4th Citizen. It is no matter; his name's Cinna! Pluck but his name out of his heart, and turn him going.   35

3d Citizen. Tear him, tear him! [*They kill him.*] Come, brands ho! firebrands! To Brutus', to Cassius'! Burn all! Some to Decius' house and some to Casca's; some to Ligarius'! Away, go!

[*Exeunt citizens with the body of Cinna.*

ACT FOUR, scene one.

(ROME. A ROOM IN ANTONY'S HOUSE.)

Enter ANTONY, OCTAVIUS, *and* LEPIDUS.

Antony. These many, then, shall die; their names are pricked.

Octavius. Your brother too must die. Consent you, Lepidus?

Lepidus. I do consent—

Octavius.   Prick him down, Antony.

Lepidus. Upon condition Publius shall not live, Who is your sister's son, Mark Antony.

Antony. He shall not live. Look, with a spot I   6 damn him.

But, Lepidus, go you to Caesar's house.

Fetch the will hither, and we shall determine

How to cut off some charge in legacies.   9

Lepidus. What, shall I find you here?

Octavius. Or here or at the Capitol. [*Exit* LEPIDUS.

Antony. This is a slight unmeritable man,   12

Meet to be sent on errands. Is it fit,

The threefold world divided, he should stand   14

One of the three to share it?

Octavius.   So you thought him,

And took his voice who should be pricked to die

In our black sentence and proscription.   17

Antony. Octavius, I have seen more days than you;

And though we lay these honours on this man

To ease ourselves of divers sland'rous loads,   20

He shall but bear them as the ass bears gold,

To groan and sweat under the business,

Either led or driven as we point the way;

And having brought our treasure where we will,

Then take we down his load, and turn him off

(Like to the empty ass) to shake his ears   26

And graze in commons.   27

35. "turn him going": send him on his way.

6. "spot": mark (made by Antony on the list).

9. "cut . . . legacies": i.e., cut down the payment promised to the people in Caesar's will.

12. "slight unmeritable": of no merit.

14. "the threefold world divided": the division of the Roman Empire into Europe, Africa, and Asia. Antony, Octavius, and Lepidus are now the triumvirs, or triple rulers. It is this triumvirate that falls out in Shakespeare's ANTONY AND CLEOPATRA.

17. "black sentence": i.e., death sentence.
"proscription": list of those proscribed, or condemned.

20. "To . . . loads": to rid ourselves of the burden of slander, i.e., Lepidus is to take the blame for some of their actions.

26. "empty": unburdened.

27. "in commons": on the public pasture.

JULIUS CAESAR

ACT IV SCENE I

only mentioned in passing, the spirit of Brutus is powerfully present throughout this scene. We are seeing the result of his earnest, selfless attempt to save Rome from tyranny. In the world of practical politics, his effort has resulted in the dictatorship of the triumvirate of Antony, Octavius, and Lepidus, and we are left in no doubt about the nature of their rule: it is cynical, bloody, and absolute. The relations between the three are also significant. Antony and Octavius are wary of one another, as well they might be. Their open contention will be the subject of another play, ANTONY AND CLEOPATRA. Antony's dismissal of Lepidus indicates that the triumvirate has nothing to do with friendship or principle; it is a naked struggle for power, in which Lepidus is but a "property." The long analogy made between Lepidus and a beast of burden also illuminates Antony's view of his fellow men: they are to be used, as he used the mob, like animals.

ACT IV SCENE II

The remaining action of the play concerns the defeat and deaths of Brutus and Cassius, and the scene is no longer in Rome. Brutus and Cassius have gone to the east to collect troops. The scene moves accordingly, first to the camp of Brutus near Sardis, in Asia Minor, and then to the plain of Philippi in Macedonia, where the final battle is fought. The scene change makes no difference, of course, on the Elizabethan stage; we need concern ourselves only with the characters and the poetry.

IV,ii begins the famous 'quarrel scene' between Brutus and Cassius, which runs through to IV,iii,143, where their reconciliation is sealed with a drink of wine. The division between the two scenes is the invention of 18th century editors (see glossary IV,iii,s.d.) and we may ignore it except for purposes of line reference. The division between the two leaders on which this scene is based is recounted by Plutarch as follows: "Brutus sent to pray Cassius to come to the city of Sardis, and went to meet him ... Now, as it commonly happeneth in great affairs between two persons, both of them having many friends, and so many captains under them, there ran tales and complaints between them. Therefore they went into a little chamber together, and bad every man avoid, and did shut the doors to them."

Octavius.   You may do your will;
But he's a tried and valiant soldier.
   Antony. So is my horse, Octavius, and for that
I do appoint him store of provender.   30
It is a creature that I teach to fight,
To wind, to stop, to run directly on,   32
His corporal motion governed by my spirit.   33
And, in some taste, is Lepidus but so.   34
He must be taught, and trained, and bid go forth:
A barren-spirited fellow; one that feeds   36
On objects, arts, and imitations
Which, out of use and staled by other men,   38
Begin his fashion. Do not talk of him   39
But as a property. And now, Octavius,   40
Listen great things. Brutus and Cassius
Are levying powers. We must straight make head.   42
Therefore let our alliance be combined,   43
Our best friends made, or means stretched;   44
And let us presently go sit in council
How covert matters may be best disclosed   46
And open perils surest answered.
   Octavius. Let us do so; for we are at the stake   48
And bayed about with many enemies;
And some that smile have in their hearts, I fear,
Millions of mischiefs.   [*Exeunt.*   51

Scene two.

(BEFORE BRUTUS' TENT NEAR SARDIS.)

Drum. Enter BRUTUS, LUCILIUS, LUCIUS, *and the army* s.d.
           TITINIUS *and* PINDARUS *meet them.*
Brutus. Stand ho!
Lucilius. Give the word, ho! and stand!
Brutus. What now, Lucilius? Is Cassius near?
Lucilius. He is at hand, and Pindarus is come   4
To do you salutation from his master.
   Brutus. He greets me well. Your master, Pindarus, 6
In his own change, or by ill officers,   7
Hath given me some worthy cause to wish   8
Things done undone; but if he be at hand,
I shall be satisfied.
   Pindarus.   I do not doubt
But that my noble master will appear
Such as he is, full of regard and honour.   12
   Brutus. He is not doubted. A word, Lucilius,   13
How he received you. Let me be resolved.   14
   Lucilius. With courtesy and with respect enough,
But not with such familiar instances   16
Nor with such free and friendly conference   17
As he hath used of old.
   Brutus.   Thou hast described
A hot friend cooling. Ever note, Lucilius,
When love begins to sicken and decay
It useth an enforced ceremony.   21
There are no tricks in plain and simple faith;
But hollow men, like horses hot at hand,   23
Make gallant show and promise of their mettle;
                    [*Low march within.*   s.d.
But when they should endure the bloody spur,

55

30. "appoint": provide.
    "store": a supply.

32. "wind": turn.

33. "corporal motion": the movement of his body.

34. "taste": measure or degree.

36. "barren-spirited": dull, lacking spirit.

36-7. "feeds ... imitations": i.e., enjoys curiosities (curious objects), artificialities, and fashions. Some editors read "abject orts" (abandoned scraps).

38. "staled": having been made stale.

39. "Begin his fashion": are newly fashionable to him.

40. "property": thing or possession.

42. "make head": raise an army.

43. "combined": strengthened.

44. "stretched": used as fully as possible.

46. "covert ... disclosed": how secret matters may be discovered.

48. "at the stake": the image is from the Elizabethan sport of bear-baiting. The bear was tied to a stake and 'bayed' about with dogs.

51. "mischiefs": hostile thoughts; the word carried a stronger meaning for the Elizabethans than it does for us.

Stage Direction "the army": on the Elizabethan stage the army would have consisted of a few actors with swords following the leaders.

4. "Pindarus": accented on the first syllable.

6. "greets me well": i.e., with a worthy representative. It has been pointed out that Brutus is always courteous to his subordinates.

7. "In ... officers": i.e., either through a change in himself, or through the fault of his officers.

8. "worthy": justifiable.

12. "regard": respect.

13. "A word": i.e., tell me.

14. "resolved": fully informed.

16. "familiar instances": signs of familiarity or friendship.

17. "conference": talk.

21. "enforced ceremony": forced politeness.

23. "hollow ... hand": insincere men, like horses who are eager at first.

Stage Direction The "march" was generally a drum offstage, and a "low march" a drum beaten softly to indicate that the approaching army was still at some distance.

ACT IV SCENE III

In Plutarch the actual quarrel between Cassius and Brutus takes very little space, but Shakespeare makes a good deal of it. Plutarch says that "they began to pour out their complaints one to the other, and grew hot and loud, earnestly accusing one another, and at length both fell a-weeping." Shakespeare's version has received a great deal of praise, and some adverse criticism. As early as 1692 Thomas Rymer wrote that the two generals resembled "two drunken Hectors huffing and swaggering for a two-penny reckoning" but Rymer wrote in an age when tragic figures were obliged to maintain an inflexible nobility at all times. Other critics, notably Bradley, have said that the incident is dra-

---

They fall their crests, and like deceitful jades 26
Sink in the trial. Comes his army on? 27
  Lucilius. They mean this night in Sardis to be
    quartered.
The greater part, the horse in general, 29
Are come with Cassius.
  Brutus.   Hark! He is arrived.
March gently on to meet him. 31
         Enter CASSIUS *and his powers.*
  Cassius. Stand ho!
  Brutus. Stand ho! and speak the word along.
  1st Soldier. Stand!
  2nd Soldier. Stand!
  3d Soldier. Stand!
  Cassius. Most noble brother, you have done me
    wrong.
  Brutus. Judge me, you gods! wrong I mine
    enemies?
And if not so, how should I wrong a brother?
  Cassius. Brutus, this sober form of yours hides 40
    wrongs;
And when you do them—
  Brutus.   Cassius, be content. 41
Speak your griefs softly. I do know you well. 42
Before the eyes of both our armies here
(Which should perceive nothing but love from us)
Let us not wrangle. Bid them move away.
Then in my tent, Cassius, enlarge your griefs,
And I will give you audience.
  Cassius.   Pindarus,
Bid our commanders lead their charges off 48
A little from this ground.
  Brutus. Lucilius, do you the like; and let no man
Come to our tent till we have done our conference.
Let Lucius and Titinius guard our door.
                         [Exeunt.

Scene three.

(WITHIN BRUTUS' TENT.)

      Enter BRUTUS *and* CASSIUS.   s.d.
  Cassius. That you have wronged me doth appear in
    this:
You have condemned and noted Lucius Pella 2
For taking bribes here of the Sardians;
Wherein my letters, praying on his side, 4
Because I knew the man, was slighted off. 5
  Brutus. You wronged yourself to write in such a case.
  Cassius. In such a time as this it is not meet
That every nice offence should bear his comment. 8
  Brutus. Let me tell you, Cassius, you yourself
Are much condemned to have an itching palm,
To sell and mart your offices for gold 11
To undeservers.
  Cassius.   I an itching palm?
You know that you are Brutus that speaks this,
Or by the gods, this speech were else your last!
  Brutus. The name of Cassius honours this cor-
    ruption,

---

26. "fall their crests": lower their manes.
    "jades": worthless horses.

27. "Sink . . . trial": fail in the test.

29. "horse in general": the cavalry.

31. "gently": slowly.

40. "sober form": restrained manner.

41. "content": calm.

42. "griefs": grievances.

48. "charges": troops.

Stage Direction Scenes two and three are always divided in editions of this play, and are here, for convenient cross-reference to other editions or critical works. The division is obviously a post-Shakespearean introduction; there is no real change of scene; Brutus and Cassius simply move to another part of the stage, or go into the inner stage.

2. "noted": publicly disgraced.

4. "letters": in Shakespeare the word is often singular in meaning.

5. "slighted off": contemptuously dismissed.

8. "nice . . . comment": trivial error should be criticized.

11. "mart your offices": i.e., make bargains or profits because of your powers.

JULIUS CAESAR

ACT IV SCENE III

matically irrelevant. This is true only if one considers the play as a chain of historical events, or a plot-sequence. The fact that so many critics have found it powerful and that audiences are always moved by it indicates that it is necessary to the development and total imaginative effect of the play. Coleridge went so far as to say that he "knew of no part of Shakespeare" that so impressed him "with the belief of his genius being superhuman."

The subject of the argument appears as soon as the two leaders are alone within the tent. Bribes have been taken from the local Sardians, and Cassius himself is suspected of having "an itching palm" in this respect. This criticism, coming from Brutus, has a twofold power. We may well imagine his attitude to the practice of taking bribes in general, and the righteous scorn in the phrase "sell and mart your offices for gold." But Brutus has another, deeper source of concern, and he goes on to make an oblique reference to it in line 18-28. We recall Brutus' anguished concern over the morality involved in joining the conspiracy against Caesar (II,i,10 ff.). There he was worried about his own motives, and honesty. More recently he has been given a painful lesson, by Antony, of the way in which professed and actual motives may differ—of the dishonesty, in short, that surrounds the struggle for power. Is the conspiracy, on which he has staked his moral being, itself corrupt? He uses the word at line 15—"The name of Cassius honours this corruption"—and goes on to address not only Cassius, but himself. His anger and the desperate, questioning quality of the speech indicate that Brutus is thinking of the moral basis of the whole enterprise, as well as the particular lapse on Cassius' part—"Did not great Julius bleed for justice sake?", "shall we now contaminate our fingers . . . sell the mighty space of our large honours?" Cassius, however, pays no attention to this line of moral self-examination. For him the attack is personal, and he rapidly brings the argument to the level of direct insult. He is, he says, the "older" and "abler" soldier—"You are not . . . I am . . . I say you are not . . . Urge me no more!" The pathos here lies in the fact that Cassius does not understand the grounds of Brutus' rage, any more than Brutus understands the way in which his contempt ("I'll use you for my mirth") wounds Cassius.

Since the part of Brutus in this play requires a continued dignity on the part of the actor, this scene is often played in such a way as to make Brutus seem above the conflict. This makes the scene

And chastisement doth therefore hide his head.
Cassius. Chastisement?
Brutus. Remember March; the ides of March remember.
Did not great Julius bleed for justice sake?
What villain touched his body that did stab
And not for justice? What, shall one of us,
That struck the foremost man of all this world
But for supporting robbers—shall we now   23
Contaminate our fingers with base bribes,
And sell the mighty space of our large honours   25
For so much trash as may be grasped thus?
I had rather be a dog and bay the moon
Than such a Roman.
Cassius.   Brutus, bait not me!   28
I'll not endure it. You forget yourself
To hedge me in. I am a soldier, I,   30
Older in practice, abler than yourself   31
To make conditions.   32
Brutus.   Go to! You are not, Cassius.
Cassius. I am.
Brutus. I say you are not.
Cassius. Urge me no more! I shall forget myself.
Have mind upon your health. Tempt me no further.
Brutus. Away, slight man!   37
Cassius. Is't possible?
Brutus.   Hear me, for I will speak.
Must I give way and room to your rash choler?   39
Shall I be frighted when a madman stares?   40
Cassius. O ye gods, ye gods! Must I endure all this?
Brutus. All this! Aye, more. Fret till your proud
    heart break.
Go show your slaves how choleric you are
And make your bondmen tremble. Must I budge?
Must I observe you? Must I stand and crouch   45
Under your testy humour? By the gods,   46
You shall digest the venom of your spleen,   47
Though it do split you; for from this day forth
I'll use you for my mirth, yea, for my laughter,
When you are waspish.
Cassius.   Is it come to this?
Brutus. You say you are a better soldier.
Let it appear so; make your vaunting true,   52
And it shall please me well. For mine own part,
I shall be glad to learn of noble men.   54
Cassius. You wrong me every way! You wrong me,
    Brutus!
I said an elder soldier, not a better.
Did I say 'better'?
Brutus.   If you did, I care not.
Cassius. When Caesar lived he durst not thus have
    moved me.   58
Brutus. Peace, peace! You durst not so have
    tempted him.
Cassius. I durst not?
Brutus. No.
Cassius. What, durst not tempt him?
Brutus.   For your life, you durst not.
Cassius. Do not presume too much upon my love.
I may do that I shall be sorry for.

23. "supporting robbers": i.e., for supporting those who would rob Romans of their liberties.

25. "the . . . honours": i.e., the great scope we have in conferring honors.

28. "bait": tempt to violence.

30. "hedge me in": restrict me.

31. "practice": experience.

32. "make conditions": to decide matters.

37. "slight": worthless.

39. "way . . . choler": scope to your anger.

40. "stares": glares or glowers with anger.

45. "crouch": bow.

46. "testy humour": irritable temper.

47. "digest . . . spleen": swallow the poison of your anger. The spleen was held to be the source of anger.

52. "vaunting": boasting.

54. "learn of": both i) discover the existence of, and ii) learn a lesson from.

58. "moved": angered.

JULIUS CAESAR

ACT IV SCENE III

weaker than it might be. Here is the view of a recent director of the play. "I would like to decry Brutus' too-often played supra-human aloofness. Far too often, in the quarrel scene, poor Cassius rages in a vacuum while Brutus stands quietly by 'playing' the honest, honourable, loftily Olympian Stoic. This is utter nonsense. Brutus is a human being. He is a powerful, determined crusader who is outraged at what he considers injustice, further infuriated by the fact that it comes from one he loves deeply, and filled with grief over the death of Portia. The storm breaks, and he flies into a towering rage, showing it with all the vigour and force of a powerful man who has had all he can take . . . at the end Cassius says 'I did not think you would have been so angry,' amazed and shaken at an impassioned scene all the more staggering because it is so rare for Brutus. BOTH men must play it to the hilt."

It is true that Brutus' righteous anger ought to be given full reign in the scene, but there is another of Brutus' qualities that Shakespeare reminds us of in a minor, subtle touch. Cassius, who is not overly scrupulous about principles, and is prosecuting the campaign as forcefully as he can has, apparently, levied funds from the surrounding country. Brutus attacks him for wringing money "from the hard hands of peasants." Brutus would himself be incapable of this kind of extortion. He is "armed so strong in honesty" that he "can raise no money by vile means." Yet it turns out (75) that Brutus has asked Cassius for money; in fact, condemning the extortion, he then asks for some of the profits. Here, as elsewhere, Shakespeare indicates that honour, nobility, and integrity are admirable, but that they are often accompanied by self-righteousness and muddle-headed thinking.

We have remarked on how many critics have praised the quarrel scene, although finding it somehow irrelevant, or pointless, in the action as a whole. Bradley remarks on the "pathos" of the scene, and says that this is an emotion that frequently occurs somewhere in the second half of a Shakespearean tragedy. There is certainly a pathetic futility in the quarrel. Perhaps the pathos lies mainly in the fact that the two leaders of the conspiracy had, but a few scenes before, been celebrating the "peace" they had brought to Rome; now they are engaged in a petty, vituperative war with one another. The scene also has the effect of showing us the two men as confused, emotional human beings, rather than as public figures.

Brutus. You have done that you should be sorry for.
There is no terror, Cassius, in your threats;
For I am armed so strong in honesty
That they pass by me as the idle wind,
Which I respect not. I did send to you
For certain sums of gold, which you denied me;
For I can raise no money by vile means.
By heaven, I had rather coin my heart
And drop my blood for drachmas than to wring
From the hard hands of peasant their vile trash
By any indirection. I did send   75
To you for gold to pay my legions,
Which you denied me. Was that done like Cassius?
Should I have answered Caius Cassius so?
When Marcus Brutus grows so covetous
To lock such rascal counters from his friends,   80
Be ready, gods, with all your thunderbolts,
Dash him to pieces!
  Cassius.   I denied you not.
  Brutus. You did.
  Cassius. I did not. He was but a fool that brought
My answer back. Brutus hath rived my heart.   85
A friend should bear his friend's infirmities,
But Brutus makes mine greater than they are.
  Brutus. I do not, till you practise them on me.
  Cassius. You love me not.
  Brutus.   I do not like your faults.
  Cassius. A friendly eye could never see such faults.
  Brutus. A flatterer's would not, though they do appear
As high as huge Olympus.
  Cassius. Come, Antony, and young Octavius, come!
Revenge yourselves alone on Cassius.
For Cassius is aweary of the world:
Hated by one he loves; braved by his brother;   96
Checked like a bondman; all his faults observed,
Set in a notebook, learned and conned by rote   98
To cast into my teeth. O, I could weep
My spirit from mine eyes! There is my dagger,
And here my naked breast; within, a heart
Dearer than Pluto's mine, richer than gold.   102
If that thou be'st a Roman, take it forth.
I, that denied thee gold, will give my heart.
Strike as thou didst at Caesar; for I know,
When thou didst hate him worst, thou lovedst him better
Than ever thou lovedst Cassius.
  Brutus.   Sheathe your dagger.
Be angry when you will; it shall have scope.   108
Do what you will; dishonour shall be humour   109
O Cassius, you are yoked with a lamb
That carries anger as the flint bears fire;
Who, much enforced, shows a hasty spark,   112
And straight is cold again.
  Cassius.   Hath Cassius lived
To be but mirth and laughter to his Brutus
When grief and blood ill-tempered vexeth him?   115
  Brutus. When I spoke that, I was ill-tempered too.
  Cassius. Do you confess so much? Give me your hand.

75. "indirection": dishonest dealing.

80. "rascal counters": cheap coins.

85. "rived": split in two.

96. "braved": defied.

98. "conned by rote": learned by heart.

102. Cassius (and Shakespeare) have here confused Pluto, the god of the underworld, and Plutus, the god of wealth.

108. "scope": freedom.

109. "dishonour . . . humour": i.e., I shall take any insult as an effect of your mood.

112. "much enforced": violently or repeatedly struck.

115. "blood ill-tempered": unbalanced emotion.

58

JULIUS CAESAR

ACT IV SCENE III

The supposedly stoical Brutus loses his self-control, and the supposedly selfish Cassius pleads for the love of his friend. This is not, as some critics have said, a lapse in dignity. It rather brings a new kind of sympathy to bear on the two men.

The reconciliation of the quarrel takes place over a glass of wine and Brutus, in a couple of laconic phrases (147), reveals the death of Portia. His iron restraint here and later in the scene on the subject of Portia's death is dramatically effective, and adds to what we already know of the man. There are several references throughout the play to Brutus' philosophy. He was a Stoic, (as distinct from the Epicurean Cassius) but Shakespeare is not particularly concerned with the technical points and assumptions of the Stoic philosophy. For him (as for most of us) the chief Stoic virtue was fortitude in the face of suffering, and this fortitude required the continual discipline of the emotions. We know of Brutus' love for Portia, and therefore a large element of the dramatic interest in this scene arises from the conflict in him between his love and his self-discipline. Since Brutus does not allow himself to speak of Portia at any length, the actor must suggest the struggle in the way he plays the scene, and some of the drama is lost in reading it. This suggests the solution to a probem that has always vexed scholars and editors at this point in the play. Brutus re-

Brutus. And my heart too.

Cassius.　　　　　　O Brutus!

Brutus.　　　　　　　　What's the matter?

Cassius. Have you not love enough to bear with me
When that rash humour which my mother gave me　120
Makes me forgetful?

Brutus.　　　　　Yes, Cassius; and from henceforth,
When you are over-earnest with your Brutus,
He'll think your mother chides, and leave you so.

Enter a poet, followed by LUCILIUS, TITINIUS, *and* LUCIUS.

Poet. Let me go in to see the generals!
There is some grudge between 'em. 'Tis not meet
They be alone.

Lucilius. You shall not come to them.

Poet. Nothing but death shall stay me.

Cassius. How now? What's the matter?

Poet. For shame, you generals! What do you mean?
Love and be friends, as two such men should be;
For I have seen more years, I'm sure, than ye.

Cassius. Ha ha! How vilely doth this cynic rhyme!　133

Brutus. Get you hence, sirrah! Saucy fellow,　134
　　hence!

Cassius. Bear with him, Brutus. 'Tis his fashion.

Brutus. I'll know his humour when he knows his
　　time.　　　　　　　　　　　　　　　　　　136
What should the wars do with these jigging fools?　137
Companion, hence!　　　　　　　　　　　　138

Cassius.　　　　　　　Away, away, be gone!

　　　　　　　　　　　　　　　　[*Exit poet.*

Brutus. Lucilius and Titinius, bid the commanders
Prepare to lodge their companies to night.

Cassius. And come yourselves, and bring Messala
　　with you
Immediately to us. [*Exeunt* LUCILIUS *and* TITINIUS

Brutus.　　　　　　Lucius, a bowl of wine.

　　　　　　　　　　　　　　　　[*Exit Lucius*

Cassius. I did not think you could have been so
　　angry.

Brutus. O Cassius, I am sick of many griefs.

Cassius. Of your philosophy you make no use
If you give place to accidental evils.　　　　　146

Brutus. No man bears sorrow better. Portia is dead.

Cassius. Ha! Portia?

Brutus. She is dead.

Cassius. How scaped I killing when I crossed　150
　　you so?
O insupportable and touching loss!　　　　　151
Upon what sickness?　　　　　　　　　　152

Brutus.　　　　　　Impatient of my absence,
And grief that young Octavius with Mark Antony
Have made themselves so strong; for with her　154
　　death
That tidings came. With this she fell distract,　155
And (her attendants absent) swallowed fire.　156

Cassius. And died so?

Brutus.　　　　Even so.

Cassius.　　　　　　O ye immortal gods!

Enter LUCIUS *with wine and tapers.*

Brutus. Speak no more of her. Give me a bowl of
　　wine.　　　　　　　　　　　　　[*Drinks.*
In this I bury all unkindness, Cassius.　　　　159

120. "rash . . . me": i.e., the quick temper I inherited from my mother.

133. "cynic": the word is used here to mean philosopher, with special reference to the school of Cynics who were generally critical of anyone else's behavior.

134. "Saucy": insolent.

136. "I'll . . . time": i.e., I'll attend to him when he chooses the proper time to speak to me.

137. "jigging": here rhyming, contemptuously.

138. "Companion": a contemptuous form of address.

146. "accidental evils": evils that come by chance.

150. "crossed": opposed.

151. "touching": grievous. The word was stronger for the Elizabethans than it is for us.

152. "Upon": as a result of.

154-5. "for . . . came": i.e., the news of their strength and her death came together.

155. "distract": out of her mind.

156. "swallowed fire": the detail is from Plutarch, who says she "cast hot burning coals into her mouth . . . and she choked herself."

159. "unkindness": enmity.

veals the death to Cassius (147) and then seems to be ignorant of it later in his talk to Messala (185). Several ingenious theories have been put forward suggesting that Shakespeare re-wrote the play, adding a second version of the Portia news, and forgetting to remove the first. Scholars and editors have a tendency to think of a Shakespeare play as a document to be read, rather than acted on a stage, and perhaps that has misled them here. Brutus' intense struggle with himself appears first with Cassius, and again with Messala. In the second occurrence he is in public, with his lieutenants, and behaves with the required Stoic control—with "meditating" on the possibility of Portia's death he has "the patience to endure it now"—and both Messala and Cassius voice their admiration for his courage. The fact that they do so indicates that the actor playing Brutus reveals an intense, continuing struggle for control, and Shakespeare has put in the two versions to give him the opportunity to do this. It is one of those examples of Shakespeare's stagecraft that we often miss in the printed text.

Cassius. My heart is thirsty for that noble pledge.
Fill, Lucius, till the wine o'erswell the cup.
I cannot drink too much of Brutus' love.
                      [Drinks. Exit LUCIUS.

          Enter TITINIUS *and* MESSALA.

Brutus. Come in, Titinius! Welcome, good Messala.
Now sit we close about this taper here
And call in question our necessities.   165
  Cassius. Portia, art thou gone?
  Brutus.   No more, I pray you.
Messala, I have here received letters
That young Octavius and Mark Antony
Come down upon us with a mighty power,
Bending their expedition toward Philippi.
  Messala. Myself have letters of the selfsame tenure. 171
  Brutus. With what addition?   172
  Messala. That by proscription and bills of outlawry 173
Octavius, Antony, and Lepidus
Have put to death an hundred senators.
  Brutus. Therein our letters do not well agree.
Mine speak of seventy senators that died
By their proscriptions, Cicero being one.
  Cassius. Cicero one?
  Messala.   Cicero is dead,
And by that order of proscription.
Had you your letters from your wife, my lord?
  Brutus. No, Messala.
  Messala. Nor nothing in your letters writ of her?
  Brutus. Nothing, Messala.
  Messala.   That methinks is strange.
  Brutus. Why ask you? Hear you aught of her in
    yours?
  Messala. No, my lord.
  Brutus. Now as you are a Roman, tell me true.
  Messala. Then like a Roman bear the truth I tell;
For certain she is dead, and by strange manner.
  Brutus. Why, farewell, Portia. We must die,
    Messala.
With meditating that she must die once,   191
I have the patience to endure it now.
  Messala. Even so great men great losses should
    endure.
  Cassius. I have as much of this in art as you, 194
But yet my nature could not bear it so.   195
  Brutus. Well, to our work alive. What do you think 196
Of marching to Philippi presently?   197
  Cassius. I do not think it good.
  Brutus.   Your reason?
  Cassius.   This it is:
'Tis better that the enemy seek us.
So shall he waste his means, weary his soldiers,
Doing himself offence, whilst we, lying still, 201
Are full of rest, defence, and nimbleness.
  Brutus. Good reasons must of force give place to
    better.
The people 'twixt Philippi and this ground
Do stand but in a forced affection;   205
For they have grudged us contribution.
The enemy, marching along by them,
By them shall make a fuller number up, 208
Come on refreshed, new added, and encouraged; 209

165. "call . . . necessities": examine our needs.

171. "tenture": meaning, information.

172. "addition?": i.e., with anything else?

173. "proscription": sentence of death. "bills of outlawry": i.e., lists of those outlawed.

191. "once": at some time.

194. "in art": in knowledge (of the Stoic philosophy).

195. "my nature": i.e., my natural emotions or instincts.

196. "alive": which concerns the living.

197. "presently": at once.

201. "offence": damage.

205. "a forced affection": loyalty compelled by force.

208. "By them": by enlisting them.

209. "new added": with new additions.

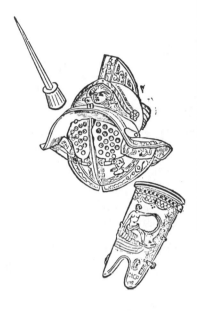

The visiting soldiers leave (238) and we enter the last phase of this long scene. It begins with a delicate touch, and again one that is more obvious in the staging than in the reading. Shakespeare frequently writes something like 'stage directions' into his lines—phrases which indicate how the actor should perform—in case the director is particularly obtuse. We have one of these at 240; Brutus' "speak'st drowsily" can only mean that Lucius yawns; it is an important detail. Lucius has earlier represented the calm and peace which Brutus, in joining the conspiracy, has lost forever (see Commentary II,i.), and here the presence of the sleepy, innocent boy, reminds us again of the other, vanished dimension of Brutus' life. This reminiscence of peace and harmony is expanded in what follows. Brutus' gentleness to the drowsy Lucius, his thoughtfulness in instructing his guards to "sleep on cushions in my tent" is evidence of his civilized humanity, just as the book he takes to read is evidence of his contemplative turn of mind. In fact much of Brutus' misunderstanding of the tactics of the conspiracy, his confident but erratic decisions, his inability to

From which advantage shall we cut him off
If at Philippi we do face him there,
These people at our back.
    Cassius.   Hear me, good brother.
    Brutus. Under your pardon. You must note beside
That we have tried the utmost of our friends,   214
Our legions are brimful, our cause is ripe.
The enemy increaseth every day;
We, at the height, are ready to decline.
There is a tide in the affairs of men
Which, taken at the flood, leads on to fortune;
Omitted, all the voyage of their life   220
Is bound in shallows and in miseries.
On such a full sea are we now afloat,
And we must take the current when it serves
Or lose our ventures.   224
    Cassius.   Then, with your will, go on.
We'll along ourselves, and meet them at Philippi.
    Brutus. The deep of night is crept upon our talk
And nature must obey necessity,
Which we will niggard with a little rest.   228
There is no more to say?
    Cassius.   No more. Good night.
Early to-morrow will we rise and hence.   230
    Brutus. Lucius! [*Enter* LUCIUS.] My gown. [*Exit*
    LUCIUS.] Farewell good Messala.
Good night, Titinius. Noble, noble Cassius,
Good night and good repose.
    Cassius.   O my dear brother,
This was an ill beginning of the night!
Never come such division 'tween our souls!
Let it not, Brutus.
               Enter LUCIUS *with the gown.*
    Brutus.   Everything is well.
    Cassius. Good night, my lord.
    Brutus.   Good night, good brother.
    Titinius, Messala. Good night, Lord Brutus.
    Brutus.   Farewell every one.
    [*Exeunt* CASSIUS, TITINIUS, *and* MESSALA.
Give me my gown. Where is thy instrument?   239
    Lucius. Here in the tent.
    Brutus.   What, thou speak'st drowsily?
Poor knave, I blame thee not; thou art o'erwatched. 241
Call Claudius and some other of my men;
I'll have them sleep on cushions in my tent.
    Lucius. Varro and Claudius!
               Enter VARRO *and* CLAUDIUS.
    Varro. Calls my lord?
    Brutus. I pray you, sirs, lie in my tent and sleep.
It may be I shall raise you by and by
On business to my brother Cassius.
    Varro. So please you, we will stand and watch 249
        your pleasure.
    Brutus. I will not have it so. Lie down, good sirs. 250
It may be I shall otherwise bethink me.   251
              [VARRO *and* CLAUDIUS *lie down.*
Look, Lucius, here's the book I sought for so;
I put it in the pocket of my gown.
    Lucius. I was sure your lordship did not give it me.
    Brutus. Bear with me, good boy, I am much forgetful.

214. "tried . . . of": tested thoroughly.

220. "Omitted": missed, not taken.

224. "ventures": investments in a voyage; the sailing metaphor is continued.

228. "niggard": be stingy with, i.e., they will sleep less than is necessary.

230. "hence": leave.

239. "instrument": in most productions Lucius plays a lute.

241. "knave": boy (affectionate). "o'erwatched": tired with watching, or being on duty.

249-50. "stand . . . pleasure": stand by and await your commands.

251. "otherwise bethink me": change my mind.

ACT IV SCENE III

see through Antony's deception, is understandable in the light of this scene. Here we have the scholarly, and in some ways un-worldly Brutus on his own. With his soldiers, he has just ordered the preparation for a battle. But on his own turns to literature and to music (see glossary I,ii,204).

Music occurs often in Shakespeare's plays. It is, in part, a relief from the strain of dialogue and action, but it has a more important dramatic function. Whether the song is happy or sad, it contributes a powerful emotional sense, or 'atmosphere' to the scene. The song here has an air of melancholy and perhaps nostalgia (see glossary s.d.) which underlines this moment of calm.

It is a particularly effective piece of stagecraft to introduce the ghost at this juncture. For a brief interlude Brutus has been at peace, but the knowledge that he has slain Caesar, and that the assassination has achieved none of its noble aims, can never be far from him. The ghost's entrance is heralded by the candle that "burns ill." This is an accordance with the Elizabethan belief that the appearance of spirits was accompanied by a wind, but it also suggests an effective modern staging. Brutus' reading is interrupted by a gust of wind, and on raising his head he sees the apparition. In the theater of today ghosts, and supernatural occurrences generally, are difficult to manage. Our audiences are accustomed to 'realistic' theater, which shows them only the sort of thing that they expect to see in everyday life. Therefore Shakespeare's ghosts on our stages are usually produced with strange lighting effects, off-stage sounds, and the like. This was not a problem for the Elizabethans, who simply accepted ghosts, just as they accepted Macbeth's witches, or his "air-born dagger." The ghost probably wore a special garment, called "a robe for to go invisible," and he was accepted as being invisible to all those on the stage who were not supposed to see him.

The ghost of Caesar is equally effective whether we imagine it to have objective reality or to be simply a creation of Brutus' exhausted mind. In either case it is a powerful and frightening manifestation of Caesar, whose presence is felt continually in the last half of the play. It had been the assumption of the conspirators that the death of Caesar would, in itself, produce a new, free Rome. Instead of this, Caesar proved to be more powerful dead than alive. His return to Brutus here is ironic, when we recall Brutus' statement that he wants only to destroy "Caesar's spirit" (II,i,169). That is exactly what he has not been able to destroy.

Canst thou hold up thy heavy eyes awhile,
And touch thy instrument a strain or two?
Lucius. Ay, my lord, an't please you.
Brutus.   It does, my boy.
I trouble thee too much, but thou art willing.
Lucius. It is my duty, sir.
Brutus. I should not urge thy duty past thy might. 261
I know young bloods look for a time of rest. 262
Lucius. I have slept, my lord, already.
Brutus. It was well done; and thou shalt sleep again;
I will not hold thee long. If I do live,
I will be good to thee.

         [*Music, and a song.* LUCIUS *falls asleep.* s.d.
This is a sleepy tune. O murd'rous slumber! 267
Layest thou thy leaden mace upon my boy, 268
That plays thee music? Gentle knave, good night.
I will not do thee so much wrong to wake thee.
If thou dost nod, thou break'st thy instrument;
I'll take it from thee; and, good boy, good night.
Let me see, let me see. Is not the leaf turned down
Where I left reading? Here it is, I think.

Enter the ghost of CAESAR.

How ill this taper burns! Ha! who comes here?
I think it is the weakness of mine eyes
That shapes this monstrous apparition.
It comes upon me. Art thou any thing? 278
Art thou some god, some angel, or some devil,
That mak'st my blood cold, and my hair to stare? 280
Speak to me what thou art.
Ghost. Thy evil spirit, Brutus.
Brutus.   Why com'st thou?
Ghost. To tell thee thou shalt see me at Philippi.
Brutus. Well; then I shall see thee again?
Ghost. Ay, at Philippi.
Brutus. Why, I will see thee at Philippi then.
                    [*Exit* GHOST.
Now I have taken heart thou vanishest.
Ill spirit, I would hold more talk with thee.
Boy! Lucius! Varro! Sirs! Awake!
Claudius!
Lucius. The strings, my lord, are false. 291
Brutus. He thinks he still is at his instrument.
Lucius, awake!
Lucius. My lord?
Brutus. Didst thou dream, Lucius, that thou so criest out?
Lucius. My lord, I do not know that I did cry.
Brutus. Yes, that thou didst. Didst thou see anything?
Lucius. Nothing, my lord.
Brutus. To sleep again, Lucius. Sirrah Claudius!
[*to* VARRO.] Fellow thou, awake!
Varro. My lord?
Claudius. My lord?
Brutus. Why did you so cry out, sirs, in your sleep?
Both. Did we, my lord?
Brutus.   Ay. Saw you anything?
Varro. No, my lord, I saw nothing.

261. "might": strength.

262. "young bloods": young constitutions.

Stage Direction The song usually sung on the stage at this point is "Orpheus with his lute," from HENRY VIII. Queen Katherine asks for it in that play when she "grows sad with troubles," and it is suitably melancholy. Another appropriate Elizabethan song that has been suggested for Lucius is John Dowland's "Come, Heavy Sleep."

267. "murd'rous": resembling death in its effect.

268. "mace": staff used by an arresting officer.

278. "upon": toward.
    "thing": i.e., material, physical thing.

280. "stare": stand up with fear. Cf. Macbeth V,iv,10-13:
    The time has been my senses would have cooled
    To hear a night-shriek, and my fell of hair
    Would at a dismal treatise rouse and stir
    As life were in 't.

291. "false": out of tune.

JULIUS CAESAR

ACT IV SCENE III

More than most of Shakespeare's plays, supernatural portents and omens abound in JULIUS CAESAR. One of the effects of these occurrences is to give us a sense of impending disaster, and that is what the ghost does here. After the brief remembrance of harmony and peace in Lucius' song, Brutus moves towards his final crisis.

ACT V SCENE I

The last Act of the play concerns the final conflict of the two factions, and here again Shakespeare rearranges and compresses the historical events he found in Plutarch to suit his own dramatic purposes. There were in fact two battles at Philippi, they were separated by about three weeks, and Octavius was not even present at the first. Shakespeare merges the two engagements into a continuous battle; and in this scene he brings Antony and Octavius face to face with Brutus and Cassius in order to contrast the two groups before the struggle begins.

Antony and Octavius appear first (1-20), and we are at once impressed with their confidence. Brutus' decision to meet them at Philippi "answers their hopes"—it is clear that Brutus has made an error here, and he is to make another (V,iii,5). Antony seems to have complete knowledge of the enemy intentions, and they are acting, he says, with "fearful bravery," or empty bravado. We are given a strong suggestion here of the desperation in the tactics of Brutus and Cassius, which will be enlarged later in the scene. We have already had sufficient opportunity to observe Antony's ruthless competence in action. Octavius now emerges a little more clearly. There a minor exchange (16-19) in which Octavius coolly but firmly asserts his equality with Antony, and later the language he uses to Brutus and Cassius leave no doubt of his confidence in his own power. It is very possible that Shakespeare, in this subtle strengthening of Octavius' character, is recalling the whole of the Antony-Octavius story as he read it in Plutarch. These two will later struggle for supremacy, with Octavius the victor, and that phase of the story will provide the plot for ANTONY AND CLEOPATRA. Although Shakespeare waited seven years before writing the later play, he seems to have Octavius' potential power in mind here.

Claudius.   Nor I, my lord.
Brutus. Go and commend me to my brother Cassius.
Bid him set on his powers betimes before,   307
And we will follow.
Both.   It shall be done, my lord   [*Exeunt.*

ACT FIVE, scene one.

(THE PLAIN OF PHILIPPI.)

Enter OCTAVIUS, ANTONY *and their army.*

Octavius. Now, Antony, our hopes are answered.
You said the enemy would not come down
But keep the hills and upper regions.
It proves not so. Their battles are at hand;   4
They mean to warn us at Philippi here,   5
Answering before we do demand of them.   6
Antony. Tut! I am in their bosoms and I know   7
Wherefore they do it. They could be content   8
To visit other places, and come down   9
With fearful bravery, thinking by this face   10
To fasten in our thoughts that they have courage.
But 'tis not so.

Enter a messenger.
Messenger.   Prepare you, generals.
The enemy comes on in gallant show;   13
Their bloody sign of battle is hung out,   14
And something to be done immediately.
Antony. Octavius, lead your battle softly on   16
Upon the left hand of the even field.
Octavius. Upon the right hand I. Keep thou the left.
Antony. Why do you cross me in this exigent?   19
Octavius. I do not cross you; but I will do so.
                                          [*March.*
Drum. Enter BRUTUS, CASSIUS, *and their army.*
LUCILIUS, TITINIUS *and others.*
Brutus. They stand and would have parley.
Cassius. Stand fast, Titinius. We must out and talk.   22
Octavius. Mark Antony, shall we give sign of battle?
Antony. No, Caesar, we will answer on their charge.   24
Make forth. The generals would have some words.   25
Octavius. Stir not until the signal.
Brutus. Words before blows. Is it so, countrymen?
Octavius. Not that we love words better, as you do.
Brutus. Good words are better than bad strokes, Octavius.
Antony. In your bad strokes, Brutus, you give good words;
Witness the hole you made in Caesar's heart,
Crying 'Long live! Hail, Caesar!'
Cassius.   Antony,
The posture of your blows are yet unknown;   33
But for your words, they rob the Hybla bees,   34
And leave them honeyless.
Antony.   Not stingless too.
Brutus. O yes, and soundless too!

307. "betimes": early in the morning, before me.

4. "battles": armies.

5. "warn": defy, oppose.

6. "Answering . . . them": attacking us before we attack them.

7. "in their bosoms": either i) I can read their thoughts, or ii) my spies are among them.

8-9. "content . . . places": would rather be elsewhere.

10. "fearful bravery": a brave appearance hiding their fear.
"face": show.

13. "gallant show": splendid array.

14. "bloody sign": red flag. Shakespeare uses this elsewhere as a sign of battle.

16. "softly": slowly.

19. "exigent": emergency.

22. "Stand fast": hold your forces here. "out": go forward.

24. "answer . . . charge": attack when they do.

25. "Make forth": i.e., let us go forward.

a

33. "posture": form or shape.

34. "Hybla bees": the bees of Mt. Hybla, in Sicily, were famous for their honey. Cassius refers to the honey of Antony's eloquence in his funeral oration.

JULIUS CAESAR

ACT V SCENE I

This sort of confrontation between leaders who are about to do battle is common in Shakespeare. Since the battle itself can be given only a restricted presentation on the stage, the hostility is dramatized at length in the dialogue as well. In this debate (27-66) we sense an element of weakness, or uncertainty, in Cassius and Brutus. The sneering comparison of Antony's eloquence to the "honey" and "buzzing" of bees (33-7) is not very apt in view of what Antony has accomplished. He is a good deal more than a troublesome insect as Brutus knows. Cassius' phrases (61-2) calling Octavius and Antony a "schoolboy" and a "reveller" come most inappropriately from a soldier who has been chased from Rome and brought to bay in Macedonia by the two men he here condescends to. On the other hand Antony's denunciation of the conspirators (39-44) is striking and vivid—we can feel his searing anger. Finally, Octavius' closing words, contemptuously inviting his enemies to fight when they feel they have sufficient courage, have the effect of leaving Brutus and Cassius distinctly at a loss as Octavius and Antony turn their backs on them and stalk off the stage.

The remainder of this scene intensifies our sense of the hopelessness of the cause of Brutus and Cassius. This is done, not by any direct statement, but through a series of suggestive speeches in which the two leaders seem to imply, in spite of themselves, that the end is near. Cassius' violent outburst (after Octavius and Antony have left) has a recklessness about it that is not far from despair. Shakespeare's characters often speak in this way when they feel the trap closing on them—we may recall Macbeth's anguished "Blow wind! Come wrack! At least we'll die with harness on our back!" The source of Cassius' desperation becomes clearer in the speech to Messala, which follows. The "mighty eagles" which had perched on his ensign would be associated with the bronze eagles which formed the standard of the mighty Roman legions: their power is replaced by the symbol of death in the scavengers who traditionally anticipated death. We also recall Cassius' earlier, scornful comment on Caesar's "superstition" (II,i, 195); now he himself expresses his belief in the "things that do presage."

For you have stol'n their buzzing, Antony,
And very wisely threat before you sting.
Antony. Villains! you did not so when your vile daggers
Hacked one another in the sides of Caesar.
You showed your teeth like apes, and fawned like hounds,
And bowed like bondmen, kissing Caesar's feet;
Whilst damned Casca, like a cur, behind
Struck Caesar on the neck. O you flatterers!
Cassius. Flatterers? Now Brutus, thank yourself!
This tongue had not offended so to-day
If Cassius might have ruled.
Octavius. Come, come, the cause! If arguing make us sweat,   48
The proof of it will turn to redder drops   49
Look,
I draw a sword against conspirators.
When think you that the sword goes up again?   52
Never, till Caesar's three-and-thirty wounds
Be well avenged, or till another Caesar   54
Have added slaughter to the sword of traitors.   55
Brutus. Caesar, thou canst not die by traitors' hands
Unless thou bring'st them with thee.
Octavius.   So I hope.
I was not born to die on Brutus' sword.
Brutus. O, if thou wert the noblest of thy strain,   59
Young man, thou couldst not die more honourable.
Cassius. A peevish schoolboy, worthless of such honour,   61
Joined with a masker and a reveller!   62
Antony. Old Cassius still.
Octavius.   Come, Antony, away!
Defiance, traitors, hurl we in your teeth.
If you dare fight to-day, come to the fields;
If not, when you have stomachs.   66
      [*Exeunt* OCTAVIUS, ANTONY, *and army.*
Cassius. Why now blow wind, swell billow, and swim bark!   67
The storm is up, and all is on the hazard.   68
Brutus. Ho, Lucilius! Hark, a word with you.
Lucilius.   My lord?
      [BRUTUS *and* LUCILIUS *talk apart.*
Cassius. Messala.
Messala.   What says my general?
Cassius.   Messala,
This is my birthday; as this very day   72
Was Cassius born. Give me thy hand, Messala.
Be thou my witness that against my will
(As Pompey was) am I compelled to set   75
Upon one battle all our liberties.
You know that I held Epicurus strong   77
And his opinion. Now I change my mind
And partly credit things that do presage.   79
Coming from Sardis, on our former ensign   80
Two mighty eagles fell; and there they perched,
Gorging and feeding from our soldiers' hands,
Who to Philippi here consorted us.   83
This morning they are fled away and gone,
And in their steads do ravens, crows, and kites   85

48. "the cause": i.e., to the business at hand.

49. "proof": trial in battle.

52. "goes up": is sheathed.

54. "another Caesar": i.e., Octavius himself.

55. "Have added slaughter": has also been killed by.

59. "strain": family.

61. "schoolboy": Octavius was twenty-one.

62. "masker and reveller": the "gamesome" quality in Antony that has been referred to at I,ii,203-4 and II,ii, 116. The Elizabethan "mask" or masque was an elaborate theatrical entertainment fashionable at court. This is another example of the minor anachronisms that gave to the ancient Rome of this play a contemporaneous, Elizabethan quality.

66. "stomachs": appetite for battle; courage.

67. "bark": a ship.

68. "on the hazard": at stake.

72. "as": as on (understood).

75. "As Pompey was": Pompey was persuaded against his judgment to fight Caesar at Pharsalia, and was defeated.

77. "held Epicurus strong": Epicurus was a Greek philosopher; as a believer in his teachings, Cassius could not have admitted the evidence of portents or omens.

79. "presage": predict.

80. "former ensign": foremost standard or banner.

83. "consorted us": accompanied us.

85. "ravens, crows, and kites": birds proverbially associated with death.

JULIUS CAESAR

ACT V SCENE I

Both Cassius and Brutus make reference to philosophy in this scene. Cassius' Epicurean view held that the mind found its chief virtue in sensible, controlled living (our sense of 'epicurean' came much later) unaffected by any sort of superstition. Brutus' Stoic view held that virtue lay in disciplined endurance. Although Shakespeare has not enlarged on their philosophical principles, he makes both men abandon their philosophies at this point. Cassius forgets his 'rational' rejection of evil portents; he now feels that they presage his death. Brutus the thinker has been opposed to suicide; but Brutus the Roman soldier will refuse to "be led in triumph" as a captive through Rome. Both men have been brooding on the likelihood of their defeat. They do not mention it directly, but this preception of defeat gives the deep poignancy to the speeches in which they say farewell "for ever and for ever" (115-121).

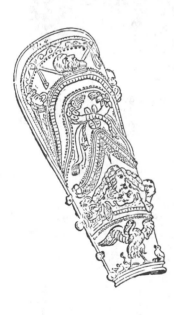

ACT V SCENE II

There is a brief silence after the farewells of Brutus and Cassius at the end of Scene i, and then the 'Alarum' sounds the battle's beginning. There is often in Shakespeare an oscillation, or see-saw, between success and failure at the crisis of the play. Here, in Brutus' brief, shouted lines, there seems a momentary chance of victory. Titinius' reveals Brutus' error at the beginning of the next scene.

Fly o'er our heads and downward look on us
As we were sickly prey. Their shadows seem 87
A canopy most fatal, under which
Our army lies, ready to give up the ghost.
  Messala. Believe not so.
  Cassius.   I but believe it partly;
For I am fresh of spirit and resolved
To meet all perils very constantly. 92
  Brutus. Even so Lucilius. 93
  Cassius.   Now, most noble Brutus,
The gods to-day stand friendly, that we may,
Lovers in peace, lead on our days to age!
But since the affairs of men rest still uncertain,
Let's reason with the worst that may befall. 97
If we do lose this battle, then is this
The very last time we shall speak together.
What are you then determined to do?
  Brutus. Even by the rule of that philosophy 101
By which I did blame Cato for the death 102
Which he did give himself—I know not how,
But I do find it cowardly and vile,
For fear of what might fall, so to prevent 105
The time of life—arming myself with patience 106
To stay the providence of some high powers 107
That govern us below.
  Cassius.   Then, if we lose this battle,
You are contented to be led in triumph 109
Through the streets of Rome?
  Brutus. No, Cassius, no. Think not, thou noble
          Roman,
That ever Brutus will go bound to Rome.
He bears too great a mind. But this same day
Must end that work the ides of March begun,
And whether we shall meet again I know not.
Therefore our everlasting farewell take.
For ever and for ever farewell, Cassius!
If we do meet again, why, we shall smile;
If not, why then this parting was well made.
  Cassius. For ever and for ever farewell, Brutus!
If we do meet again, we'll smile indeed;
If not, 'tis true this parting was well made.
  Brutus. Why then, lead on. O that a man might
          know
The end of this day's business ere it come!
But it sufficeth that the day will end,
And then the end is known. Come, ho! Away!
                    [*Exeunt.*

Scene two.

(THE BATTLEFIELD.)

Alarum. Enter BRUTUS *and* MESSALA. s.d.
  Brutus. Ride, ride, Messala, ride, and give these bills 1
Unto the legions on the other side.   [*Loud alarum.* 2
Let them set on at once; for I perceive
But cold demeanour in Octavius' wing, 4
And sudden push gives them the overthrow. 5
Ride, ride, Messala! Let them all come down. 6
                    [*Exeunt.*

87. "sickly": sickening, about to die.

92. "constantly": with fortitude.

93. "Even so Lucilius": Brutus finishes the conversation he has been having, aside, with Lucilius.

97. "Let's reason with": let's examine.

101. "that philosophy": the Stoic philosophy in which suicide was considered cowardly.

102. for Cato's death see note at II,i,295.

105-6. "to prevent The time of life": to anticipate the termination of life.

107. "to . . . providence": to await the judgment.

109. "led in triumph": led as a captive in the triumphal procession.

Stage Direction "Alarum": a conventional signal, on either trumpets or drums, summoning an army to battle.

1. "bills": orders.

2. "the other side": the other flank of the army, commanded by Cassius.

4. "cold demeanour": lack of fighting spirit.

5. "gives . . . overthrow": i.e., will overthrow them.

6. "Let . . . down": command the whole army to come down from the heights.

This scene exhibits another simple but effective Shakespearean method for representing a battle within the limitations of the Elizabethan stage. Cassius, whose eyesight is "thick" orders Pindarus to the upper stage—representing a point "higher on that hill"—and in their tense exchange we follow the progress of Titinius.

Brutus' glimmer of hope in Scene ii is seen to be illusory. Cassius' soldiers are defeated by Antony. While Brutus is successful against Octavius he is not able to help Cassius, thus indirectly bringing about Cassius' death. It is ironic that it should be the soldiers of the honest Brutus who "fall to spoil," and, in their looting and plundering, fail to help the forces of Cassius. But it is a further and greater irony that Cassius, who has always perceived the practical realities of the situation around him, is now finally and fatally misled by his servant's report. The presentation of Cassius has changed subtly but drastically in the course of the play, how much so we can see if we recall the soliloquy which closed I,ii. There Cassius, driven by envy and hatred, was a subtle, scheming Machiavellian. But the Cassius of the quarrel scene was a man of dignity, sensitivity, and human warmth. And in a series of details since then (e.g., the belief in portents, the rumination of his birthday, the farewell to Brutus) Shakespeare shows another side to Cassius. This is in part for dramatic reasons. Until the assassination the unscrupulous Cassius and the honest Brutus were in dramatic contrast; after the assassination the conflict and contrast is largely between Antony and the conspirators. But there is no real inconsistency in Shakespeare's presentation of Cassius. The conspirator of the first half of the play has become the hunted Roman patriot of the second half. Shakespeare simply reveals another aspect of the man, and one which adds pathos to his death. Cassius has predicted before in this play that he will take his own life, and now, as he does, he is able to remark on the irony of the act: Caesar's murderer has become his revenger.

Scene three.

(THE BATTLEFIELD.)

Alarum. Enter CASSIUS *and* TITINIUS.

Cassius. O look, Titinius, look! The villains fly!   1
Myself have to mine own turned enemy.   2
This ensign here of mine was turning back;   3
I slew the coward and did take it from him.   4
Titinius. O Cassius, Brutus gave the word too early,   5
Who, having some advantage on Octavius,
Took it too eagerly. His soldiers fell to spoil,   7
Whilst we by Antony are all enclosed.

Enter PINDARUS.

Pindarus. Fly further off, my lord! Fly further off!
Mark Antony is in your tents, my lord.
Fly therefore, noble Cassius, fly far off!
Cassius. This hill is far enough. Look, look, Titinius!
Are those my tents where I perceive the fire?
Titinius. They are, my lord.
Cassius.   Titinius, if thou lovest me,
Mount thou my horse and hide thy spurs in him
Till he have brought thee up to yonder troops
And here again, that I may rest assured
Whether yond troops are friend or enemy.
Titinius. I will be here again even with a thought.   [*Exit.*

Cassius. Go, Pindarus, get higher on that hill.
My sight was ever thick. Regard Titinius,   21
And tell me what thou not'st about the field.
                    PINDARUS *goes up.*   s.d.
This day I breathed first. Time is come round,
And where I did begin, there shall I end.
My life is run his compass. Sirrah, what news?
Pindarus. [*Above.*] O my lord!
Cassius. What news?
Pindarus. [*Above.*] Titinius is enclosed round about
With horsemen that make to him on the spur.   29
Yet he spurs on. Now they are almost on him.
Now Titinius! Now some light. O, he lights too!   31
He's ta'en. [*Shout.*] And hark! They shout for joy.
Cassius. Come down; behold no more.
O coward that I am to live so long
To see my best friend ta'en before my face!

Enter PINDARUS *from above.*

Come hither, sirrah.
In Parthia did I take thee prisoner;
And then I swore thee, saving of thy life,   38
That whatsoever I did bid thee do,
Thou shouldst attempt it. Come now, keep thine oath.
Now be a freeman, and with this good sword,
That ran through Caesar's bowels, search this bosom.   42
Stand not to answer. Here, take thou the hilts;   43
And when my face is covered, as 'tis now,
Guide thou the sword. [PINDARUS *stabs him.*] Caesar
      thou art revenged
Even with the sword that killed thee.   [*Dies.*
Pindarus. So, I am free; yet would not so have been,

---

1. "villains": i.e., his own men.

2. "to mine own": against my own (men).

3. "ensign": standard-bearer.

4. "it": i.e., the standard itself.

5. "the word": i.e., the word to attack.

7. "spoil": looting, pillage.

21. "thick": dim, not clear.

Stage Direction "goes up": Pindarus leaves the main stage and re-appears on the balcony, or upper stage, which then represents "that hill."

29. "make . . . spur": i.e., gallop toward him, spurring their horses.

31. "light": dismount.

38. "swore . . . life": i.e., I made you take an oath, as a condition of letting you live.

42. "search": probe, pierce.

43. "Stand not": don't delay.

JULIUS CAESAR

ACT V SCENE III

Titinius' and Messala's lines 51-60 are difficult on the modern stage where the actors would be immediately aware of Cassius' body as they entered. Granville-Barker reminds us of the depth of the Elizabethan stage to justify a moment of search: "Stage direction is embodied in dialogue. We have the decelerated arrival telling of relief from strain, the glance round the seemingly empty place; then the sudden swift single-syllabled line and its repetition, Titinius' dart forward, Messala's graver question, the dire finality of the answer."

Shakespeare's dramatic concentration of the two battles of Philippi into one leads him into a minor error. Titininus remarks on the setting sun (60) and yet Brutus, since another engagement is to come, has to announce that it is three o'clock in the closing lines of the scene. Shakespeare is careless about this kind of slip because it makes no real difference to what he is trying to do on the stage, which is to create a poetic effect. The pathos of the deaths of Cassius and Titinius is given poetic statement by Brutus. A recent editor says of his closing speech: "Brutus, however, hopes to live and triumph. The play approaches its climax as does a solemn movement of a symphony. The rhythm quickens momentarily, offering a tentative hope of a return to a happier theme. Then chord after chord leads to the tragic close" (F. A. Ferguson).

Durst I have done my will. O Cassius!
Far from this country Pindarus shall run,
Where never Roman shall take note of him.   [*Exit.*
        Enter TITINIUS *and* MESSALA.

Messala. It is but change, Titinius; for Octavius 51
Is overthrown by noble Brutus' power,
As Cassius' legions are by Antony.
  Titinius. These tidings will well comfort Cassius.
  Messala. Where did you leave him?
  Titinius.   All disconsolate,
With Pindarus his bondman, on this hill.
  Messala. Is not that he that lies upon the ground?
  Titinius. He lies not like the living. O my heart!
  Messala. Is not that he?
  Titinius.   No, this was he Messala,
But Cassius is no more. O setting sun,
As in thy red rays thou dost sink to night,
So in his red blood Cassius' day is set!
The sun of Rome is set. Our day is gone;
Clouds, dews, and dangers come; our deeds are done!
Mistrust of my success hath done this deed. 65
  Messala. Mistrust of good success hath done this
    deed.
O hateful Error, Melancholy's child, 67
Why dost thou show to the apt thoughts of men 68
The things that are not? O Error, soon conceived,
Thou never com'st unto a happy birth,
But kill'st the mother that engendered thee! 71
  Titinius. What, Pindarus! Where art thou,
    Pindarus?
  Messala. Seek him, Titinius, whilst I go to meet
The noble Brutus, thrusting this report
Into his ears. I may say 'thrusting' it,
For piercing steel and darts envenomed
Shall be as welcome to the ears of Brutus
As tidings of this sight.
  Titinius.   Hie you, Messala,
And I will seek for Pindarus the while.
                  [*Exit* MESSALA.
Why didst thou send me forth, brave Cassius?
Did I not meet thy friends, and did not they
Put on my brows this wreath of victory 82
And bid me give it thee? Didst thou not hear their
    shouts?
Alas, thou has misconstrued everything! 84
But hold thee, take this garland on thy brow.
Thy Brutus bid me give it thee, and I
Will do his bidding. Brutus, come apace
And see how I regarded Caius Cassius. 88
By your leave, gods. This is a Roman's part. 89
Come, Cassius' sword, and find Titinius' heart.
              [*Stabs himself and dies.*
Alarum. Enter BRUTUS, MESSALA, YOUNG CATO,
STRATO, VOLUMNIUS *and* LUCILIUS.
  Brutus. Where, where, Messala, doth his body lie?
  Messala. Lo, yonder, and Titinius mourning it.
  Brutus. Titinius' face is upward.
  Cato.   He is slain.
  Brutus. O Julius Caesar, thou art mighty yet!
Thy spirit walks abroad and turns our swords
In our own proper entrails.   [*Low alarums.* 96

51. "change": i.e., one thing for another.

65. "my success": the result of my mission.

67. "Melancholy's child": i.e., those that are melancholy are mistaken in their judgment.

68. "apt": ready to receive any impression.

71. "mother": i.e., the melancholy person who conceived the error.

82. "wreath": a laurel wreath.

84. "misconstrued": with the accent on the second syllable.

88. "regarded": honored.

89. Titinius asks the gods to allow him to take his life before the time they have allotted him.
"part": role.

96. "own proper": very own.

ACT V SCENE IV

This brief scene of battle is a prelude to the final defeat. The action on the stage will be as vigorous and brutal as possible, with Cato's death and Lucilius' capture signifying the final destruction of Brutus' forces. Death is here sought after as an honor, and Lucilius attempts to die in the place of Brutus, and to show his devotion to him. Shakespeare takes the incident from Plutarch: "Lucilius seeing a troop of barbarous men going all together right against Brutus, he determined to slay them with the hazard of his life, and being left behind, told them that he was Brutus . . . Lucilius was brought to Antonius, and stoutly with a bold countenance said: Antonius, I dare assure thee, that no enemy hath taken nor shall take Marcus Brutus alive."

The scene suggests the loyalty and courage that Brutus inspires. It also contrasts the hopelessness of Brutus' cause with the confident, secure directions with which Antony ends the scene.

Cato.   Brave Titinius!
Look whe'r he have not crowned dead Cassius.   97
  Brutus. Are yet two Romans living such as these?
The last of all the Romans, fare thee well!
It is impossible that ever Rome
Should breed thy fellow. Friends, I owe moe tears   101
To this dead man than you shall see me pay.
I shall find time, Cassius; I shall find time.
Come therefore, and to Thasos send his body.   104
His funerals shall not be in our camps,
Lest it discomfort us. Lucilius, come;   106
And come, young Cato. Let us to the field.
Labeo and Flavius set our battles on   108
'Tis three o'clock; and, Romans, yet ere night
We shall try fortune in a second fight.   [*Exeunt.*

Scene four.

(THE BATTLEFIELD.)

Alarum. Enter BRUTUS, MESSALA, YOUNG CATO, LUCILIUS *and* FLAVIUS.
Brutus. Yet, countrymen, O yet hold up your heads!
              [*Exit* BRUTUS, MESSALA *and* FLAVIUS.
Cato. What bastard doth not? Who will go with me?   2
I will proclaim my name about the field.
I am the son of Marcus Cato, ho!   4
A foe to tyrants, and my country's friend.
I am the son of Marcus Cato, ho!
              Enter soldiers and fight.   s.d.
Lucilius. And I am Brutus, Marcus Brutus I!   7
Brutus, my country's friend! Know me for Brutus!
                        [YOUNG CATO *falls.*
O young and noble Cato, art thou down?
Why, now thou diest as bravely as Titinius,
And may'st be honoured, being Cato's son.
1st Soldier. Yield, or thou diest.
Lucilius.   Only I yield to die.   12
There is so much that thou wilt kill me straight.   13
Kill Brutus, and be honoured in his death.
1st Soldier. We must not. A noble prisoner!
              Enter ANTONY.
2nd Soldier. Room ho! Tell Antony Brutus is ta'en.
1st Soldier. I'll tell the news. Here comes the
    general.
Brutus is ta'en! Brutus is ta'en, my lord!
Antony. Where is he?
Lucilius. Safe, Antony; Brutus is safe enough.
I dare assure thee that no enemy
Shall ever take alive the noble Brutus.
The gods defend him from so great a shame!
When you do find him, or alive or dead,
He will be found like Brutus, like himself.   25
Antony. This is not Brutus, friend; but, I assure you,
A prize no less in worth. Keep this man safe;
Give him all kindness. I had rather have
Such men my friends than enemies. Go on,
And see whe'r Brutus be alive or dead;
And bring us word unto Octavius' tent
How every thing is chanced.   [*Exeunt.*   32

97. "whe'r": whether.

101. "thy fellow": your equal.
"moe": more.

104. "Thasos": an island near Philippi where Plutarch says that Cassius was buried.

106. "discomfort us": dishearten our troops.

108. "battles": troops.

2. "What bastard": i.e., who is so low born that...

4. "Cato": see note at ll,i,295.

Stage Direction The actors were accomplished fencers, and the battles dramatically exciting. One of the few contemporary references to the play recalls how the audience were "ravished" by the actors "on the Stage at halfe-sword parley."

7. Plutarch says that Lucilius impersonated Brutus, apparently in order to draw off the enemy.

12. "Only . . . die": I surrender only that I may die.

13. "so much": i.e., Brutus' power is such that he must be killed at once.

25. "like himself": true to himself.

32. "is chanced": has happened.

Shakespeare takes the details of Brutus' death from Plutarch. "Now the night being far spent, Brutus as he sat, bowed towards Clitus one of his men, and told him somewhat in his ear: the other answered him not, but fell weeping. Thereupon he proved Dardanus . . . and at length Volumnius, praying him that he would help him to put his hand to his sword, to thrust it in him to kill him. Volumnius denied his request, and so did many others . . . Then Brutus taking every man by the hand, he said these words unto them with a cheerful countenance . . . It rejoiceth my heart, that not one of my friends have failed me; as for me, I think myself happier than those that have overcome, considering that I leave a perpetual fame of our courage and manhood."

Shakespeare so arranges the scene that stage directions for "alarums" add a growing note of urgency to Brutus' requests. Octavius and Antony are closing in. We have watched Brutus through a long succession of reverses, in which his noble motives became continually entangled with and frustrated by the realities of the world of political and military action. But the simple statement at lines 34-8 remind us of the direct, honest, uncomplicated character that he is. He does "have glory by this losing day" in a sense in which his opponents can never have it in their victory.

Brutus' dying reference to Caesar indicates again the force that the dead Caesar has exerted through the second half of the play. Caesar alive may have been pompous, tyrannical and cruel. Caesar dead, "the spirit of Caesar" that Brutus tried to destroy, has been all-powerful. Antony's bloody prophecy, made over his body, has been fulfilled. He was present in the minds (and language) of the conspirators when they quarreled. His ghost, appearing to Brutus, heralded the final movement of the action. Cassius died with Caesar's name on his lips and Brutus, finding Cassius dead, spoke lines which sum up the action of the play: "O Julius Caesar, thou art mighty yet! /Thy spirit walks abroad and turns our swords/In our own proper entrails."

In most of Shakespeare's tragedies there comes, at the play's end, a brief, final moment of calm. The conflict of the play has run its course, the hero is dead, and there is usually a speech which concludes the action on a quiet, elegaic note. Here the speech is given to Antony, and it is a moving tribute to Brutus' qualities. There is no need to question

Scene five.

(THE BATTLEFIELD.)

Enter BRUTUS, DARDANIUS, CLITUS, STRATO *and* VOLUMNIUS.

Brutus. Come, poor remains of friends, rest on this 1
rock.

Clitus. Statilius showed the torchlight; but my lord, 2
He came not back. He is or ta'en or slain.

Brutus. Sit thee down, Clitus. Slaying is the word.
It is a deed in fashion. Hark thee, Clitus.

[*Whispers.*

Clitus. What, I, my lord? No, not for all the world!

Brutus. Peace then. No words.

Clitus.   I'll rather kill myself.

Brutus. Hark thee, Dardanius. [*Whispers.*

Dardanius.   Shall I do such a deed?

Clitus. O Dardanius!

Dardanius. O Clitus!

Clitus. What ill request did Brutus make to thee?

Dardanius. To kill him, Clitus. Look, he meditates.

Clitus. Now is that noble vessel full of grief, 13
That it runs over even at his eyes.

Brutus. Come hither, good Volumnius. List a word.

Volumnius. What says my lord?

Brutus.   Why this, Volumnius.
The ghost of Caesar hath appeared to me
Two several times by night—at Sardis once, 18
And this last night here in Philippi fields.
I know my hour is come.

Volumnius.   Not so, my lord.

Brutus. Nay, I am sure it is, Volumnius.
Thou seest the world, Volumnius, how it goes.
Our enemies have beat us to the pit. 23

[*Low alarums.*

It is more worthy to leap in ourselves
Than tarry till they push us. Good Volumnius,
Thou know'st that we two went to school together.
Even for that our love of old, I prithee
Hold thou my sword-hilts whilst I run on it.

Volumnius. That's not an office for a friend, my 29
lord [*Alarums still.* s.d.

Clitus. Fly, fly, my lord! There is no tarrying
here.

Brutus. Farewell to you; and you; and you,
Volumnius.
Strato, thou hast been all this while asleep.
Farewell to thee too, Strato. Countrymen,
My heart doth joy that yet in all my life
I found no man but he was true to me.
I shall have glory by this losing day
More than Octavius and Mark Antony
By this vile conquest shall attain unto.
So fare you well at once; for Brutus' tongue 39
Hath almost ended his life's history.
Night hangs upon mine eyes; my bones would rest,
That have but laboured to attain this hour. 42

[*Alarum. Cry within* 'Fly, fly, fly!'

1. "poor remains": pitiful remains.

2. "the torchlight": a detail taken from Plutarch, who recounts how a scout penetrated Cassius' camp, then occupied by Antony, and tried to signal to Brutus' forces.

a

13. "vessel": person, here imagined as filled with tears.

18. "several": separate.

23. "to the pit": i) a hole in which an animal is trapped, ii) grave.

29. "office": service.

Stage Direction "still": continuing, increasing in intensity.

39. "at once": all together.

42. "That . . . hour": the line may mean i) I have striven only to attain this honorable death, or ii) I have experienced only pain in attaining my death.

JULIUS CAESAR

ACT V SCENE V

Antony's consistency here. The passions of the struggle have gone; and Antony and Octavius both speak here, not so much as particular characters, but as representative Romans mourning a dead hero without reference to political faction.

Clitus. Fly, my lord, fly!

Brutus.   Hence! I will follow.

  [*Exeunt* CLITUS, DARDANIUS, *and* VOLUMNIUS.

I prithee, Strato, stay thou by thy lord.

Thou art a fellow of a good respect;   45

Thy life hath had some smatch of honour in it.   46

Hold then my sword, and turn away thy face

While I do run upon it. Wilt thou, Strato?

Strato. Give me your hand first. Fare you well, my lord.

Brutus. Farewell, good Strato. [*Runs on his sword.*] Caesar, now be still.

I killed not thee with half so good a will.   [*Dies.*

  Alarum. Retreat. Enter OCTAVIUS, ANTONY,   s.d.
    MESSALA, LUCILIUS *and the army.*

Octavius. What man is that?

Messala. My master's man. Strato, where is thy master?

Strato. Free from the bondage you are in Messala.

The conquerors can but make a fire of him;   55

For Brutus only overcame himself,   56

And no man else hath honour by his death.

Lucilius. So Brutus should be found. I thank thee, Brutus,

That thou hast proved Lucilius' saying true.   59

Octavius. All that served Brutus, I will entertain 60
them.

Fellow, wilt thou bestow thy time with me?

Strato. Ay, if Messala will prefer me to you.   62

Octavius. Do so, good Messala.

Messala. How died my master, Strato?

Strato. I held the sword, and he did run on it.

Messala. Octavius, then take him to follow thee,

That did the latest service to my master.   67

Antony. This was the noblest Roman of them all.

All the conspirators save only he

Did what they did in envy of great Caesar;

He only, in a general honest thought   71

And common good to all, made one of them.   72

His life was gentle, and the elements   73

So mixed in him that Nature might stand up   74

And say to all the world, 'This was a man!'

Octavius. According to his virtue let us use him, 76

With all respect and rites of burial.

Within my tent his bones to-night shall lie,

Most like a soldier, ordered honourably.   79

So call the field to rest, and let's away   80

To part the glories of this happy day.   [*Exeunt.* 81

45. "respect": repute.

46. "smatch": touch.

Stage Direction "Retreat": sounded by the trumpets to signal the end of a battle.

55. "make a fire": cremate.

56. "Brutus only overcame": only Brutus overcame.

59. "Lucilius' saying": at V,iv, 21-25.

60. "entertain": take them into my service.

62. "prefer": recommend.

67. "latest": last.

71-2. "general . . . all": i.e., with honorable motives, and for the good of all Romans.

73. "gentle": in the old sense of noble.

73-4. "elements So mixed": qualities so balanced.

76. "use": treat.

79. "ordered honourably": treated in an honorable manner.

80. "field": those in the field of battle, the armies.

81. "part": share.

NOTES

NOTES